Between Innocence and Peace

Favourite Poems
of Ireland

Between Innocence and Peace

Favourite Poems
of Ireland

Chosen and Introduced
by

Brendan Kennelly

MERCIER PRESS

Mercier Press
PO Box 5, 5 French Church Street, Cork
24 Lower Abbey Street, Dublin 1

© Introduction & Selection Brendan Kennelly

A CIP is available for this book from the British Library.

To Meg

Printed in Ireland by Colour Books Ltd.

Contents

Introduction   9
Innocence: *Patrick Kavanagh*   13
The Finding of Moses: *Zozimus*   13
Seals at High Island: *Richard Murphy*   14
Deer's Cry: *St Patrick*   16
The Ould Orange Flute: *Anonymous*   18
I Saw from the Beach: *Thomas Moore*   20
The Midnight Court: *Brian Merriman (trans. C Ó Cuinn)*   20
The Wild Old Wicked Man: *W B Yeats*   63
The Curse: *J M Synge*   65
Queens: *J M Synge*   65
The Journey: *Eavan Boland*   66
Envoi: *Eavan Boland*   69
Fair and Forty: *Rosemarie Rowley*   70
Dear Dark Head: *Anonymous*   71
Dicey Reilly: *Anonymous*   71
Donall Oge: *Anonymous*   72
Lapis Lazuli: *W B Yeats*   74
The Ballad of William Bloat: *Raymond Calvert*   76
Biddy Mulligan: *Seamus Kavanagh*   77
The Yellow Bittern: *Cathal Buidhe Mac Elgun*   78
Bold Phelim Brady, The Bard of Armagh: *Anonymous*   79
The Boyne Water: *Anonymous*   80
The Wearin' o' the Green: *Anonymous*   82
Croppies Lie Down: *Anonymous*   83
Cockles and Mussels: *Anonymous*   84
The Sash my Father Wore: *Anonymous*   85
I Know where I'm Going: *Anonymous*   86
Return and no Blame: *Paula Meehan*   87
The Maid of the Sweet Brown Knowe: *Anonymous*   88
Molly Bawn and Brian Oge: *Anonymous*   89
The Description of an Irish Feast: *Jonathan Swift*   91
On a Curate's Complaint of Hard Duty: *Jonathan Swift*   94
Swift's Epitaph: *W B Yeats*   94
Boolavogue: *Patrick Joseph McCall*   95
An Elegy on the Death of a Mad Dog: *Oliver Goldsmith*   96
from The Deserted Village: *Oliver Goldsmith*   97
The Street: *John B. Keane*   103
The Minstrel Boy: *Thomas Moore*   104
Believe Me, if all Those Endearing Young Charms: *Thomas Moore*   105
The Last Rose of Summer: *Thomas Moore*   105
The Song of Fionnuala: *Thomas Moore*   106
Between: *Micheal O'Siadhail*   107

The Old Story over again: *James Kenney* 107
Woman: *Eaton Stannard Barrett* 108
John Kinsella's Lament for Mrs Mary Moore: *W B Yeats* 108
The Belfast Cockabendy: *Anonymous* 109
Section XVI from Autumn Journal: *Louis MacNiece* 112
Love Song: *George Darley* 114
The Burial of Sir John Moore: *Charles Wolfe* 114
Come Back, Paddy Reilly: *Percy French* 115
What will you do, Love?: *Samuel Lover* 117
The Low-backed Car: *Samuel Lover* 118
Hy-Brasail – the Isle of the Blest: *Gerald Griffin* 120
Lines Addressed to a Seagull: *Gerald Griffin* 121
The Irish Emigrant: *Lady Dufferin* 122
Throwing the Beads: *Sean Dunne* 123
My Life, My Voice, My Story: *Davoren Hanna* 123
The Nameless One: *James Clarence Mangan* 124
Gone in the Wind: *James Clarence Mangan* 126
Shapes and Signs: *James Clarence Mangan* 127
Siberia: *James Clarence Mangan* 128
Carrigafoyle: *The O'Rahilly* 129
The Mountains of Mourne: *Percy French* 133
The Bells of Shandon: *Father Prout* 134
Bad Luck to this Marching: *Charles James Lever* 135
Lament for the Death of Thomas Davis: *Samuel Ferguson* 136
The Battle Eve of the Brigade: *Thomas Davis* 138
The Little Black Rose: *Aubrey de Vere* 140
Galway Races: *Anonymous* 140
The Man from God-Knows-Where: *Florence Wilson* 141
The Rose of Tralee: *William Pembroke Mulchinock* 144
The Dying Girl: *Richard D'Alton Williams* 145
The Coolun: *Maurice O'Dugan* 147
The Redemptorist: *Austin Clarke* 148
First Autumn Night: *Katie Donovan* 149
Dark Rosaleen: *Owen Roe MacWard* 151
To the Oaks of Glencree: *J M Synge* 153
A Question: *J M Synge* 153
A Dream: *William Allingham* 154
Lovely Mary Donnelly: *William Allingham* 155
The Jewish Bride: *Paul Durcan* 156
The Man of the North Countrie: *Thomas D'Arcy M'Gee* 158
Like Dolmens Round my Childhood, the Old People: *John Montague*
158
Ode: *Arthur O'Shaughnessy* 160
A Disused Shed in Co. Wexford: *Derek Mahon* 161
An Ulsterman: *Lynn Doyle* 163
John-John: *Thomas MacDonagh* 164
Ulster Names: *John Hewitt* 166
The Man Upright: *Thomas MacDonagh* 167

Máire my Girl: *John Keegan Casey*   169
Poem : *Seamus Heaney*   170
Dread: *J M Synge*   170
The Orange Lily-o: *Anonymous*   171
The Croppy Boy: *William B McBurney(Carroll Malone)*   172
The Cry of the Dreamer: *John Boyle O'Reilly*   173
A White Rose: *John Boyle O'Reilly*   174
The Ballad of Reading Gaol: *Oscar Wilde*   175
Dublin Girl, Mountjoy 1984: *Dermot Bolger*   195
The Witch: *Katherine Tynan Hinkson*   195
Buying Winkles: *Paula Meehan*   197
The Little Waves of Breffny: *Eva Gore-Booth*   198
I will go with my Father a-Ploughing: *Joseph Campbell*   198
To my Daughter Betty, the Gift of God: *Thomas M Kettle*   199
The Dead at Clonmacnois: *Angus O'Gillan*   199
Ballad to a Traditional Refrain: *Maurice Craig*   200
Wounds: *Michael Longley*   201
The Wayfarer: *Patrick Pearse*   202
Party Shrine: *Thomas McCarthy*   203
Letter to a British Soldier on Irish Soil: *Patrick Galvin*   203
Protestant Boys: *Anonymous*   205
The Lundys Letter: *Gerald Dawe*   207
Claudy: *James Simmons*   208
The Mystery: *Amergin*   209
The Killing of Dreams: *Michael Hartnett*   210
Peace: *Patrick Kavanagh*   210
Acknowledgements   212

Introduction

Over the years, I've come to believe a few things about poetry, and the writing and reading of it. Firstly, it doesn't really matter who writes poetry; but it matters greatly that poetry be written. Secondly, there is something increasingly boring in the cosy, chronological arrangement of poetry in anthologies. We work hard to make time and its productions as cautious and predictable as our own lives, whereas time is, in fact, a wild horse that nobody has managed to tame. Let's recognise that, at least. Such a recognition prepares the way for moments of enjoyable anarchy, for fun, contrast, juggling, intensity, juxtaposition and surprise, those astonishing, and astonishingly revealing states that increasingly attract and engage me in poetry. Dull, heavy-footed, solemn-faced old time bullies a lot of decent souls into boredom. Why not, in making an anthology for one's friends and enemies, simply get rid of it? Or at least give it a cheeky kick in the pants?

This anthology is called *Between Innocence and Peace* because that, I fancy, is how many people might like to view the course of their lives. Between innocence and peace. God alone knows what lies between; but men and women will suffer and enjoy that daily mystery of comedy and tragedy, of work, boredom, banality and occasional wonder. Between innocence and peace; we lose the one and long for the other. This anthology is poised, at different levels, between loss and desire.

Fun, contrast, intensity, juxtaposition, surprise; that is what I have aimed at. I've thrown tedious old chronology out the window and am glad to be able to report that it's having the whale of a time for itself out there in the street where roving gangs of aspiring teenage rapists and some lovers of poetry come and go. (It's amazing how even the life of a street can reflect one's careful little plan for an anthology; well, a man makes plans and God laughs.)

Meanwhile, Saint Patrick, weary perhaps of wearing that

rather heavy breastplate, is taking a few lessons on (or from?) the Ould Orange Flute; Oliver Goldsmith rubs shoulders with John B. Keane (I always suspected that those two lovable and charming gentlemen would get on like a pair of houses on fire); Yeats and his 'old bawd' enjoy a chin-wag with the Belfast Cockabendy; and the Orange Lily-o is bringing a welcome splash of colour into the confessional life of the Croppy Boy. There's nothing like poetry to give you a new slant on history. And new slants, fresh perspectives, are what reading is all about.

Above all, perhaps, I have not followed any fashion. Fashion, as I have observed it in both life and literature, is another name for slavery of a rather sad, uptight kind. I have simply chosen poems that give me a thrill or a laugh, poems that sing clouds or sunlight into my heart, poems that I'm glad to read again and again for a whole host of reasons and/or for very small, unimportant, private reasons.

The anthology doesn't try to prove anything. Perhaps it shows that poetry is always capable of surprising us, if we can give it even half a chance.

And this is not merely an anthology. It amounts to an epic poem about Ireland, written by many poets living and dead. Irish poets are always trying to write *one* poem, but never quite manage to do so. This is it. This is an epic picture in which you'll see what you're capable of seeing. Enjoy it.

The book begins and ends with poems, 'Innocence' and 'Peace', by Patrick Kavanagh. Why? I love his work. It's as fresh today as when I stumbled across it forty or more years ago. Time and again Kavanagh wrote out of humility and achieved sublimity. His two poems are like an angel's wings folded about this book. But the demons and killers have their say as well. Heaven and Hell are everywhere in Ireland. So is Purgatory. And Limbo.

They're all here: sad poems, mad poems, funny poems, lonely poems, poems that demonstrate and celebrate the partitioned culture of Ireland, poems by and about women, poems that tell lies beautifully and truths clumsily, poems that sing the pains and joys of history, that tell of spiritual desolation, physical desire, remorse, love, myth, exile, homesickness, hatred, dreams, prejudice, nightmares, superstition, illness, health, war, religion, disaster and death. And all, all between innocence and peace.

There are many other poems I'd like to have included. But this'll do for now.

BRENDAN KENNELLY

Innocence

They laughed at one I loved –
The triangular hill that hung
Under the Big Forth. They said
That I was bounded by the whitethorn hedges
Of the little farm and did not know the world.
But I knew that love's doorway to life
Is the same doorway everywhere.

Ashamed of what I loved
I flung her from me and called her a ditch
Although she was smiling at me with violets.

But now I am back in her briary arms
The dew of an Indian summer morning lies
On bleached potato-stalks –
What age am I?

I do not know what age I am,
I am no mortal age;
I know nothing of women,
Nothing of cities,
I cannot die
Unless I walk outside these whitethorn hedges.

Patrick Kavanagh

The Finding of Moses

On Egypt's banks, contagious to the Nile
The Ould Pharaoh's daughter, she went to bathe in style.
She took her dip and she came unto the land,
And to dry her royal pelt she ran along the strand.
A bulrush tripped her whereupon she saw
A smiling baby in a wad of straw;

13

She took him up and says she in accents mild
'Oh taranagers, girls, now, which of yis owns the child?'

She took him up and she gave a little grin
For she and Moses were standing in their skin,
'Bedad now,' says she, 'it was someone very rude
Left a little baby by the river in the nude.'
She took him to her ould lad sitting on the throne
'Da,' says she, 'will you give the boy a home?'
'Bedad now,' says he, 'sure I've often brought in worse.
Go my darlin' daughter and get the child a nurse.'

An oul blackamore woman among the crew
Cried out 'You royal savage, what's that to do with you?
Your royal ladies is too meek and mild
To beget dishonestly this darling little child.'
'Ah then,' says Pharaoh, 'I'll search every nook
From the Phoenix Park down to Donnybrook
And when I catch hoult of the bastard's father
I will kick him from the Nile down to the Dodder.'

Well they sent a bellman to the Market Square
To see if he could find a slavey there
But the only one now that he could find
Was the little young one that left the child behind.
She came up to Pharaoh, a stranger, mareyah,
Never lettin' on that she was the baby's ma.
And so little Moses got his Mammy back
Shows that co-in-ci-dence is a nut to crack.

Zozimus

Seals at High Island

The calamity of seals begins with jaws.
Born in caverns that reverberate
With endless malice of the sea's tongue
Clacking on shingle, they learn to bark back

In fear and sadness and celebration,
The ocean's mouth opens forty feet wide
And closes on a morsel of their rock.

Swayed by the thrust and backfall of the tide,
A dappled grey bull and a brindled cow
Copulate in the green water of the cove.
I watch from a cliff-top, trying not to move.
Sometimes they sink and merge into black shoals;
Then rise for air, his muzzle on her neck,
Their winged feet intertwined as a fishtail.

She opens her fierce mouth like a scarlet flower
Full of white seeds; she holds it open long
At the sunburst in the music of their loving;
And cries a little. But I must remember
How far their feelings are from mine marooned.
If there are tears at this holy ceremony
Theirs are caused by brine and mine by breeze.

When the great bull withdraws his rod, it glows
Like a carnelian candle set in jade.
The cow ripples ashore to feed her calf;
While an old rival, eyeing the deed with hate,
Swims to attack the tired triumphant god.
They rear their heads above the boiling surf,
Their terrible jaws open, jetting blood.

At nightfall they haul out, and mourn the drowned,
Playing to the sea sadly their last quartet,
An impoverished requiem that ravishes
Reason, while ripping scale up like a net:
Brings pity trembling down the rocky spine
Of headlands, till the bitter ocean's tongue
Swells in their cove, and smothers their sweet song.

Richard Murphy

Deer's Cry

'Patrick made this hymn. It was made in the time of Loeguire (Leary) son of Niall. The cause of its composition, however, was to protect him and his monks against deadly enemies that lay in wait for the clerics. And this is a corslet of faith for the protection of body and soul against devils and men and vices. Patrick sang this when the ambuscades were laid against his coming by Loeguire, that he might not go to Tara to sow the faith. And then it appeared before those lying in ambush (Loeguire's men) that they (Patrick and his monks) were wild deer with a fawn (Benen) following. And its name is "Deer's Cry".'

Modern scholars and translators say that the hymn as handed down in its present form is not earlier than the late seventh or early eighth century; that the language in which the poem is written is of that period. The hymn is also known as 'Patrick's Breastplate'.

I arise today
    Through a mighty strength, the invocation of the Trinity,
    Through belief in the threeness,
    Through confession of the oneness
    Of the Creator of Creation.

I arise today
    Through the strength of Christ's birth with His baptism,
    Through the strength of His crucifixion with His burial,
    Through the strength of His resurrection with His ascension,
    Through the strength of His descent for the Judgment of Doom.

I arise today
    Through the strength of the love of the Cherubim,
    In obedience of angels,
    In the service of archangels,
    In hope of resurrection to meet with reward,
    In prayers of Patriarchs,
    In predictions of Prophets,
    In preachings of Apostles,
    In faiths of confessors,
    In innocence of holy Virgins,

In deeds of righteous men.

I arise today
Through the strength of heaven:
Light of sun,
Radiance of moon,
Splendour of fire,
Speed of lightning,
Swiftness of wind,
Depth of sea,
Stability of earth,
Firmness of rock.

I arise today
Through God's strength to pilot me:
God's might to uphold me,
God's wisdom to guide me,
God's eye to look before me,
God's ear to hear me,
God's word to speak for me,
God's hand to guard me,
God's way to lie before me,
God's shield to protect me,
God's host to save me
From snares of devils,
From temptations of vices,
From every one who shall wish me ill,
Afar and anear,
Alone and in a multitude.

I summon today all these powers between me and those evils,
Against every cruel, merciless power that may oppose my body and my soul,
Against incantations of false prophets,
Against black laws of pagandom,
Against false laws of heretics,
Against craft of idolatry,
Against spells of women and smiths and wizards,

Against every knowledge that corrupts man's body and
  soul.

Christ to shield me today
Against poison, against burning,
Against drowning, against wounding,
So that there may come to me abundance of reward.
Christ with me, Christ before me, Christ behind me,
Christ in me, Christ beneath me, Christ above me,
Christ on my right, Christ on my left,
Christ when I lie down, Christ when I sit down, Christ
  when I arise,
Christ in the heart of every man who thinks of me,
Christ in the mouth of every one who speaks of me,
Christ in every eye that sees me,
Christ in every ear that hears me.

I arise today
Through a mighty strength, the invocation of the Trinity,
Through belief in the threeness,
Through confession of the oneness
Of the Creator of Creation.
> *Domini est salus. Domini est salus. Christi est salus,*
> *Salus tua, Domine, sit semper nobiscum.*

Amen.

St Patrick (Attributed seventh century)
Translations of Whitney Stokes, John Strachan and Kuno Meyer

The Ould Orange Flute

In the county Tyrone, in the town of Dungannon,
Where many a ruction myself had a han' in.
Bob Williamson lived, a weaver by trade
And all of us thought him a stout Orange blade,
On the twelfth of July as around it would come
Bob played on the flute to the sound of the drum,

You may talk of your harp, your piano or lute
But there's nothing compared to the ould Orange flute.

But Bob the deceiver he took us all in,
For he married a Papish called Brigid McGinn,
Turned Papish himself, and forsook the old cause
That gave us our freedom, religion and laws.
Now the boys of the place made some comment upon it,
And Bob had to fly to the Province of Connacht
He fled with his wife and his fixings to boot,
And along with the latter his ould Orange flute.

At the chapel on Sundays, to atone for past deeds,
He said Paters and Aves and counted his beads,
Till after some time, at the priest's own desire,
He went with his ould flute to play in the choir.
He went with his ould flute to play for the Mass,
And the instrument shivered and said: 'Oh alas!'
And blow as he would, though it made a great noise.
The flute would play only 'The Protestant Boys'.

Bob jumped, and he started, and got in a flutter,
And threw his ould flute in the blest Holy Water;
He thought that this charm would bring some other
    sound
When he blew it again, it played 'Croppies lie down';
And for all he could whistle, and finger, and blow,
To play Papish music he found it no go;
'Kick the Pope', 'The Boyne Water', it freely would
    sound,
But one Papish squeak in it couldn't be found.

At the Council of priests that was held the next day,
They decided to banish the ould flute away
For they couldn't knock heresy out of its head
And they bought Bob a new one to play in its stead.
So the ould flute was doomed and its fate was pathetic,
'Twas fastened and burned at the stake as heretic,
While the flames roared around it they heard a strange
    noise –

'Twas the ould flute still whistling 'The Protestant Boys'.
Anonymous

I Saw from the Beach

I saw from the beach, when the morning was shining,
A bark o'er the waters move gloriously on;
I came when the sun o'er that beach was declining,
The bark was still there but the waters were gone.

And such is the fate of our life's early promise,
So passing the spring-tide of joy we have known;
Each wave, that we danc'd on at morning, ebbs from us,
And leaves us, at eve, on the bleak shore alone.

Ne'er tell me of glories, serenely adorning
The close of our day, the calm eve of our night –
Give me back, give me back, the wild freshness of morning,
Her clouds and her tears are worth evening's best light.

Oh, who would not welcome that moment's returning,
When passion first wak'd a new life through his frame,
And his soul, like the wood, that grows precious in burning,
Gave out all its sweets to love's exquisite flame.

Thomas Moore

The Midnight Court

I choose the river path, where feet
In dewy grasses cool their heat,
Through a tree-fledged glen I edge my way,
Made by the daylight brisk and gay.
Then my heart brightens into eyes
That see to where the Lough Gréine lies.
Earth, land and circumambient air
Are mirrored in its waters fair.
The mountain ranges row on row

A formidable beauty show,
Purple above and green below.
The withered heart, long filled with pain
Or feelingless, will trill again,
And bitter paupers, penniless,
Will quite forget their wretchedness,
When they take time to stop and stare
Over the green tree-tops to where,
Amid the mistless waters clear,
The awkward squads of ducks look queer
As, slipping through their midst, a swan
Leads them majestically on.
Fish full of fun jump one perch high,
Their speckled bellies catch my eye.
Lake-waters sport upon the shore
And raise a great gay blue-waved roar.
On merry boughs the loud birds sing,
Near me the deer mid green shaws spring
I hear the huntsmen's horn and hail,
I see hounds bound at Reynard's tail.
Oh, yestermorn did not betray
Dawn's promise of a cloudless day
When Cancer topically let fly
A tropic day in late July,
Fresh from night's rest, the sun could play
At work, and burn all in its way,
But did not strike and had not found me
Where treeleaves wrapped the green flag round me.
The grasses, shamrocks, and the clovers
In swathes embraced me like green lovers,
Each growing herb and flowering spray
Drove every worrying thought away.
World-weariness sleep-overweighed
Down flat on that green mat I laid,
Had breath enough to utter 'ugh'
And sight enough to see a shough
Or ditch by trees by which I dropped,
Stretched out my legs, got my neck propped,
Screened off the flies as best one may,

And closed both eyes, to float away
Close-clasped in slumber-clouds of grey.
A frightful nightmare maelstrom there
Took me and shook me like a cur
Gutted, cut up and plucked me bare.
Meanwhile, anaesthetised by slumber,
My empty body lay like lumber.
Then, as I dreamt, I felt the quake,
That shook the whole wide world awake,
An Arctic blast, mid flames and roars,
Raped savagely the sheltered shores.
I thought to snatch a cautious glance
And saw along the shore advance
A Brobdignagian mass – the bone
The rump – the stomach far outthrown –
Fierce features – each one on its own
Was tough enough to stand alone.
Not having a theodolite
I had to estimate her height
Six, seven yards, but eight not quite.
Six feet of cloak she did not tuck
But let go draggling through the muck.
She looked then condescendingly
But most intimidatingly
As down from a great wild wide brow she
Shed rugged, ruptured dignity
With a ragged grin from rusty teeth,
Would scare a shire or blast a heath.
Heavens! What an arm! And to beseem it
A staff huge as a weaver's beam. It
Upheld a brass spike and brass plate
Inscribed with the certificate
Of a BUMBAILIFF's powers and state.
    'Up, drowsy dodger, don't siest
Or ditch-mitch now when thousands rise
To crowd into our great Assize.
No court which rules by force alone,
No robber-court like those you've known.
The justice on the bench shall be

Sent hither from the gentle Sí
This court will hear with sympathy
The poor, the weak, the womanly,
Whose case can claim the victory.
The faery peers who discuss
The Irish problem, unlike us
Unite and are unanimous.
They've met, for two days and one night,
Upon the magic-mountain height
Where the Magh Gréine faery dwell,
Palaced in space invisible.
It grieves his faery majesty,
And all his followers bond and free,
And all the royal family,
And all the courtiers, to see
Ireland in such adversity.
Her ancient aristocracy
Have lost, by loss of property,
Their freedom to be powers that be.
No case judge they, no rent demand,
Nor may hold military command.
The land, of healthy growths bereft
Has only weeds and ruins left.
True quality melts out of view
Displaced by the rich parvenu.
That treacherous thief who thinks it play
To strip the poor he makes his prey.
Misrule and cruel violence
Are legalised at small expense
There in the dark behind the fence,
While helpless victims seek relief,
And litigate, to come to grief.
Lawyers lie low, it pays to lie,
The bench jeers down from up on high.
Deceit and partiality
Make the false evidence agree;
When unjust laws distort the mind
What verdict can a jury find
Whom bribes and fears and falsehoods blind?

'But Truth shall come out and not spare
And by the Bible I declare
It will find guilt out everywhere
That you are guilty, 'twill aver,
And must this day due justice taste
For letting your mouth go to waste;
Conduct which as you must recall
Has made the population fall.
Whole country districts far and wide
Are emptied by the ebbing tide,
And wars and plagues, still free to act,
Are never ceasing to subtract,
And proud kings, longing to be great,
Make men enlist and emigrate.
Meanwhile you young men do not mate,
You youths refuse to propagate!

'Shame on you males who, sonless, stand
And do not answer the demand
While women swarm on sea and land,
Sleek buxom fillies fit for stud,
All young hot healthy flesh and blood,
While others suffer from the slump,
Thin, listless without breast or rump,
Or slim and stately once, grow plump.
'Tis sad to think they'll never marry
Or have a healthy child to carry,
'Tis sad to think they'll never swell
In belly and in breasts as well!
Most of them wait there eagerly
Yet, bless them, oh so patiently;
Speak but the word and you will see
Them drop like ripe fruit from the tree.

'Responsible Councils of State
Discuss reports – at any rate
Ours did, at length, early and late,
But not so as to procrastinate.
Their Special Envoy has in fact
Arrived, plenipotent to act.
The dice is thrown, she is to be

24

Your ally aleatory,
Aoibheall, the genius of Craig Léith
Munster's true friend and strength and stay,
Arrived by the first flight today,
Sent by the sages of the Sí,
The Liberator who shall free
Thomond from chains of slavery.
Beauty and justice fruit and flower
In her, in promises with power;
All unjust laws she'll abrogate
When she begins to legislate,
A bulwark to support the weak
And make the violent mild and meek.
From now I vow you shall not see
Laws made by force and trickery,
No longer shall the pimp and whore
Drive through the law their coach and four,
Heaven's justice now shall judge once more.
In Fiacal the Assizes are
And you must answer at the bar,
Up, run, for you're under arrest
Make no excuse, don't dare protest.
Quick march, or else I'll have your blood
And drag you thither through thick mud!'
    With that she gaffed me through the coat –
Collar, and set off at a trot
Down one, and up another, glen
To puff up on Cnoc Maonmhaí: then
Fiacal Church gable was the spot
At which I from her pikestaff shot.
I really saw, or so 't would seem,
A spacious, stately palace gleam
Under the torchlit floodlight's stream,
Massive and lofty, full of light,
With walls and portals richly dight
With trophies of the hunt and fight.
I saw how to the bench there came
A gracious, stately Fairy Dame,
I saw the numerous bodyguard

25

On either side stand on their ward,
I saw in full house an immense
And chiefly-female, audience.
A young, angelic Maid saw I
Soft skinned and languorous of eye,
Her silk-soft lips were sweet and tender,
Her hands and fingers long and slender.
She shook, as she stood up to swear,
A lovely mass of ringlets fair,
Her hair in yellow swathes hung down,
Fierce troubles made her face one frown,
Eyes, by resentment sent ablaze,
Whetted to a sharp edge her gaze.
Sobs racked her first and words were lost,
In speechless heat her bosom tossed,
'Twas clear she wished that she were dead
Such heavy floods of tears she shed.
Straight as an arrow, with her head
Up, in the witness box she stands,
Clenches her toes or wrings her hands.
She sobbed and moaned and hiccuped till
Sighs showed that she had wept her fill.
The dark cloud scattered, then, like smoke
Out in a smile her beauty broke,
She dried her eyes and thus she spoke:
'A míle fáilte now say we
Most heartily we welcome thee,
O Aoibheall, in this evil day
Thou ancient sibyl of Craig Léith,
Our riches and our light find we
In prison and in slavery.
Tír Lorc and Thomond sigh to see
You leave the joyous host to free
Us all and bring us victory.
Hear now why I am so distraught
By woe and grief, and overwrought,
Burnt, till a vapour in the air
I go astray I know not where.
Young women flee from worldliness

26

With such unlimited excess,
And all the finest girls I know
Out of this world aspire to go,
Renouncing hope of spouse or son
Each wears black clothes and knows no one
And for no crime thought of, or done,
Condemns herself to be a nun.
    'I have in these my travels too
Met women in their hundreds who,
Were they but asked, would gladly mate;
I am, like them, quite desperate
Yet, like them I say "no", not "yes"
To spinsterhood and childlessness
Alas, shall sadness ne'er surcease
For gladness, gaiety and peace,
Must gloom and misery fill the night
Spent without sleep or sweet delight,
Without soft peace to shed its balm;
To be condemned as I now am
To tumble in a tepid bed
And struggle with my thoughts instead.
Hear, gracious lady, and redress
The grievances which we express,
We Irishwomen must confess
If the men go on the way they do,
Then we, the weaker sex, must woo,
Or start to capture and pursue!
When they to thoughts of wedlock wake
They're creatures that no girl would take,
Old, worn-out wrecks whose strength is shed
And not worth going with to bed.
    'Through youth's rash heat sometimes I own
Exceptions – one in seven – are known
Yet boys whose beards have scarcely grown
Will never choose the girl they wed
For being cultured or well bred,
Or for her figure or her face,
Nor yet, because with easy grace
She suits her charm with actions fit

27

Whether she stand or walk or sit.
They go for those most overdressed
And those who paint their faces best,
Some ugly blonde or dark brown hag,
Who has no charm of which to brag
Except a well-filled money bag.

    'It pricks my heart and sends a train
Of puzzling problems through my brain.
I'm sick and worn with all the strain,
Sobs tear me while the tears rain.
I see the sturdy, healthy blade,
Young, manly, handsome and well made,
The gay, the gentle and the kind,
The men of sense, the wise of mind,
Those who know how and when to act
Who show unerring grace and tact,
The men determined and efficient
In all things formidably proficient
At this one point prove insufficient.
See then the women whose persistence
Has made such men give up resistance!
Each, for the rest of his existence,
Condemned to cherish with his life
Some elderly or witless wife.
A slut whose head is full of nits
And stops and starts and pets and fits.
There in ill-tempered ease she sits
Yet she finds time to snoop and lurk
And give long lectures on the work
That he must do and she may shirk.
He's caught a tartar and a turk.
And I too find it most unfair,
What should be mine has gone to her.
Ochón! That ill-bred wether there,
That old ewe with the young-lamb air
With unwashed feet and uncombed hair
Wedded tonight, that burns and breaks me,
What's wrong with me that no one takes me?

    'I'm better looking far than she,

I'm neat and trim and mannerly,
Yet no one falls in love with me.
My lips may well display the row
Of pearl-white teeth which my smiles show,
I have a pretty face I know,
My eyes are bright, my brow like snow,
My eyes are grey, my waving hair
Coils in thick tresses rich and rare,
My chin and cheek unblemished shine,
Frank modesty's in every line.
My hands and fingers, throat and bosom
Win beauty prizes and can't lose 'em.
Although small boned, light as a feather
No match-stick knees knock I together.
My waist is slender yet take note
I have beneath my petticoat
A comely body well designed
And a kallipygian behind
And it's no shame to say you'll find
My legs well-shaped and well-aligned
What's best of all I won't repeat
It is a mystery complete.

 'I have good curves, I'm white of skin,
Not short and thick, or long and thin,
No sullen slut all girns and frowns,
No hanger for unironed gowns,
No óinseach either who, poor thing,
Catches fresh acne every spring.
Oh you'd go far before you could
See a piece of young womanhood
More full of spirit and red blood.

 'Were I like others that I know
Who dowdier and yet dowdier grow,
Ignorant, listless, and slow,
Too blind to mind that none regards,
Too dull, too shy, to play their cards;
Why then I'd have to give up hope,
Let go, and slither down the slope.

 'But no one's ever seen me yet

In any place where men are met,
Or any spot where young and old
Ever a wake or funeral hold,
No match or race or dance there's been
Where throngs assemble on the green,
At which I've let myself be seen
Except well-dressed, from head to foot,
In clothes all chosen well to suit,
Just enough powder on my head,
On which a well-starched coif I spread,
And over that a hood of white
Graced with a set of ribbons bright.
The printed frock I wear I deck
With ruffs both at the wrist and neck
My scarlet cloak you'll rarely view
Without some aery facing new.
A faery queen might envy me
This linen apron which, you see,
Is covered with embroidery
Of plant and herb and bird and tree.
I've sharp stiletto heels with screws
To lift the insteps of my shoes.
Buckles, silk gloves and rings add grace
To hoops and bracelets and old lace.
   'No, don't think I've been backward, I
Am not unnaturally shy,
I've never kept myself from sight as
Would some poor trembling anchoritess.
I enter and I leave a place
With curtsies elegant with grace
And dignity of brow and face,
I'm fit to be seen everywhere,
I need not draw back when men stare.
I surely put myself on show,
To every hurling green I go,
To every bonfire, romp and gambol
To race and dance and match and ramble,
To every market-day and fair,
To Mass on Sunday I repair.

I go there to be seen by men,
If any are worth seeing then
They see me look, and look again.
In spite of all my bright attractions
And all my enterprising actions,
In spite of all my love, content
To offer much encouragement
They fooled and left me in the lurch,
Not one would go with me to church.
I spent my wits in that vain search.
Yet I'd tried hard, and spent as well,
For fortunes such as tea-leaves tell
Or tinker wives with cards can spell,
A fortune – but it was all a sell.
    'I tried all tricks, I played all tunes
By waxing or by waning moons
At Shrove and at All Hallows' tide.
At feasts such as our holy guide,
The Church, does through the year provide
My many games I vainly tried.
I'd pillow my head every night
Upon a fruit-packed stocking tight,
(Emblem of that fertility
Which seems, alas, not meant for me).
All Lent I fasted piously
And slimmed myself industriously
I dipped my slip against the stream
Yet did not of a husband dream
I swept beneath the cornstack too,
Hair, nailparings in greeshugh threw,
The flail did on the hearth-stone lie,
My distaff in our limekiln I
Put; when the neighbours were not by,
I put my ball of yarn in theirs,
Yet nothing happens, no one cares.
Flax seed about our "street" I spread,
And wrapped in straw a cabbage head
To be beneath mine in the bed.
Of every trick of which I tell

Some Devil's name would make a spell
Impregnant with the powers of hell.
    'The sum and substance of my tale
Is that I tried all but to fail –
I haven't caught the sought-for male.
Here, where long history has brought me,
I read the grievous lesson taught me.
The creeping years that now have caught me
And hold me fast speed fast away.
I am not far off from the day
When I'll grow withered, old and grey.
I've not had one proposal, I
Fear I'll have none before I die.
    'Let my soul live, O hear my cries
For help, thou Pearl from Paradise.
Let me to no dim spinster fade
Nor be a meaningless old maid
Without her man to give protection,
Or child or friend to lend affection,
Huddled beside the fire, now grown
Unused to visitors, alone.
'Od's blood and thunder I declare
While lightning fills with wrath the air
I'm the poor fool left dangling there
To see the dregs that wed the cream,
All Ireland's ugliest daughters seem
To have their every wish and dream.
Saive has young fatty as her groom
Muireann now plans one young man's doom,
Mairsile and Mór live blissfully
And poke a lot of fun at me,
Sheila and Slaney feel life's good.
Cicely and Anne bring up their brood
– all th' other women have their will,
While I remain a maiden still,
Unfertilised and unpossessed,
Nursing no baby at my breast.
    'I've shown long patience, but in vain
Weak yet persistent I remain

Sure of the cure I've power to gain,
Seeking a philtre for my pain.
Liquors from dried-up herbs I wring
Which like myself, are withering.
Such druid spells shall surely bring
Some handsome lad or stripling free
At last to fall in love with me.
I've often seen it done e're this,
The recipes don't ever miss;
Sliced apples, powdered herbs have powers
To couple couples at all hours,
Magairlín meidhreach brings to view
What men and mandrakes have and do
And I'd be gladly gone into
As half of one or one of two.
Old druid aphrodisiacs
Thus make one beast that has two backs;
And other plants too I could name
Though some might think it ill became
My female modesty to mention
Either the means or the intention.
Leaves burnt with a mysterious spell
And other fearsome doings fell
I've used – but no, I must not tell.
      'North Munster's wonder was aroused
To see one single spinster spoused.
She told me what she had to do,
I swore to keep it secret too,
So don't let on that I've told you:
From Shrove right on to Hallow's tide
When she at last was made a bride
She never ate a single bite
(Her yellow hair turned almost white)
And drank a gruesome grog
(Such as would sicken any dog
Or turn the stomach of a hog,)
Brewed out of blowflies from the bog.
Long patience learns to look askance
On credit, give a cash advance

Of full and swift deliverance;
Or else, unless your visitation
Can cure my furious desperation
I'll find some desperate remedy
I'll strike and shall not spare, you'll see,
Even though it may go hard with me.'

Then an old fellow full of rage
Leaped to the centre of the stage,
Though he was bent and spent with age,
His fury from that bag of bones
And whistling chest's asthmatic groans
Shook bellows out, as in loud tones
He, to a court contemptuous
Delivered testimony thus:
'All ill and sorrow on you be,
Slut, risen up from misery.
No wonder all our suns grow dim,
No wonder Ireland's plight is grim
That misdrawn laws make wrong of right,
That justice is gone out of sight,
Our cows won't calve, their udders dry,
Evils increase and multiply,
The past was bad, the future's worse,
And then to swell the country's curse
The Mórs and Sheilas ease their passions
For dresses in the latest fashions.
        'You useless huzzy, we all know
The old manureheap whence you grow,
Just nothing on your family tree
But lags and bugs and baggery.
We know your father for a louse
That crawls about from house to house,
No cash, no credit at his call,
No backing but the nearest wall.
He's nothing in his thin grey head
But th' insects which make it their bed.
He has no "kitchen" and no bread.
He never ate food off a plate,

His clothes are in a loathsome state,
His legs of trousers show their lack
His feet are bare but polished black,
He wears no coat upon his back,
Only a súgán and a sack.
Believe, good people, if we were
To sell such creatures at a fair,
And put him up with dam and brats,
And anyone would buy the rats,
And pay the VAT too – my thought faints,
By all the bodies of the saints,
'Twould not produce, I surely think,
Enough to give you one long drink!

   'Your sort of girl of course enjoys
Making folk talk – you're a big noise,
And all the country's wondering how
A pauper without sheep or cow
Is as well dressed as you are now.
You've a silken cloak and it is well seen
That that handkerchief you wave is clean
For it's never as yet been soiled by use,
Oh! you've buckles of silver in your shoes,
And your outer covering is well designed
And that dazzling bonnet has us all blind
But I have an eye that can see behind
And I beg to state though I hate to shock
That that back of yours is without a smock.

   'Aye, even the man with the messiest mind
Will hardly guess at what we will find,
The cambric sleeve and the costly ruff
Make him too much, but not quite enough,
No! No! No corset and no stays
Will there be beneath to meet his gaze,
All the underclothing you've underneath
Is a clumsy homemade canvas sheath!
The country sees the outward things,
The tasseled gloves, the costume rings,
Cheap finery put on to hide
The red, chapped hands there are inside!

What sort of wine stands on your table?
That I'll reveal if you're unable,
It's bad potatoes that you eat
That are as dirty as your feet.
I hope they give you indigestion,
But let's turn to another question.
    'Your hair-dos do show easy grace,
And many make-ups give you face,
But don't you air that high-horse head,
For I've seen where you make your bed.
No sheet, not even one coarse-spun thread
Of blanket, quilt, or coverlet,
Only a ragged mattress set
On the earth-floor, full of your wet
In a dark filthy cabin where
There is no stool, bench, seat or chair.
The water wells up from the ground,
And drips down from the walls all round,
And if it rains, one's really drowned.
– The roof's still there, the shower to catch,
Though weeds grow thin in rotten thatch,
All paths and holes that lean hens scratch,
Though couples sag, and ridge poles slip,
And rafters have begun to dip,
The roof's still up, to drop and drip
Or, if a rainstorm comes, to drown
All in a torrent of dark brown!
    'By all the Prophets and the saints,
She's us all deaved with these complaints.
But whence come they, the dyes, the paints,
The stylish fashionable air,
The fine silk cloak she has to wear.
Ah, arra musha, I declare
I never saw a thing so quare
Such clothes upon the likes of her
And that sophisticated air,
Where did you get them, tell me where,
Tell me, you besom, if you dare?
Bought, paid for honestly? Well prove

That if you can, meanwhile I'll move
The hint that you got them for – love.
You hadn't seed to sow one inch
Until your bottom felt the pinch.
You draw your hood up and you frown
And look through your long lashes down:
How did you get that hood and gown?
Your petticoat need not appear –
It's had its ups and downs I fear –
I have no wish now to accuse –
So I'll leave your feet to open views
Of that which earned them that pair of shoes ...

A AOIBHEALL CHEANNASACH CHARTHANACH
    CHÓMHACHTACH,
GUÍM THÚ, GAIRIM THÚ, FREAGAIR IS FÓIR MÉ!

(Those orchestrated Gaelic words
Whirr pungently like thunderbirds,
The English version is, when heard,
A thing insipid and absurd.)

– O gentle strength, by mighty deeds
Succour thy suppliant's crying needs!
Such predators as she, in truth,
Have made a prey of Erin's youth.
    'On this, dear friends, I give my hand
With an example near at hand,
My neighbour in the next townland
(Not me, I trust you'll understand),
A simple lad, whose careless will
Was innocent of any ill
With one of these does once collide
And heigh ho, presto, she's his bride.
It scalds my heart to see how she
Manoeuvres so successfully,
All pride and all false dignity
Controls the barley and the cattle
And makes the gold and silver rattle.
I saw her only yesterday

37

By the roadside, and in her way
She's a fine woman, big and gay
All jokes and jeers and do and dare
Backed by a lot of derrière.
  'Far be it from me to backbite
Or stir up jealousy and spite,
But if I wished I could give fact,
Report and detail most exact
Of the way in which her skirts and she
Were tumbled and disorderly
Split in the middle on the ground
While crowds shouted and jeered all round,
Sometimes in stables on the hay,
Sometimes on public rights of way.
Tales of the unselfish gallantry
Which made her public property
Men will tell in days yet to be
Over Hybracken's wine and bread,
Where Tirmacallen's champaigns spread,
And on through Inch and Bansha then,
O'er many a hill, down many a glen,
On to Kilbracken, Clare, and Quin;
Need I be tedious, and put in
How Tradray's bean-fed legions boast
And argue which one had her most,
And how one hears no name but hers
Among the Cratley cordwainers?
  'But don't let's go too far. What's said
Let us forget and treat as dead;
But I gave her up to roast or freeze
Or catch venereal disease
When, hard by Gárus, my eye fell
Upon a public spectacle
Upon the open road all bare
Under a Doora turfcutter
And she with nothing under her ...
  'Stop thinking and take off your hat
For I am going to tell you what
Will knock you as it knocked me flat.

She who looked slim and maidenly
When she was all men's property
Could, when she wished, look matronly;
Wished for a baby and had one,
Once grace was said, the power was won
And 'twas no sooner thought than done.
The candles on the altar stated
That issue was legitimated
From when Christ's *Ego vos* began
To join that woman to one man,
Though that 'twas done no one could know
Till nine months and one week could show
It in two breasts with milk aflow.

    'What dangers threaten liberty
When wedlock locks till death sets free
Alas, perplexed and jealous state
A lad a lass he's mad to mate
To learn at last, alas, too late
Lessons experience must learn
Beyond the point of no return!

    'I'd be well off still had I known
And had gone on living alone.
I was (this district used to own
Wealthy and generous to lend
Hand, ear and welcome to a friend)
With learned friends in court to fight
My case and prove my black was white,
And other learned friends that led
The applause I thought my speech had bred
(Since wealth and land proved what I'd said)
I lived in peace and satisfaction
Right up to my one foolish action,
Done for the woman who at length
Robbed me of life and health and strength.

    'A pleasing female figure, graced
By charm of movement fitly placed,
Her bosom, bones and waist were good
And moved one, even when she stood.
Her hair ran back in waves and swirls

That twisted into corkscrew curls,
A rosy flush beneath the skin
Lit up her cheek as from within.
Her youth and smiles seemed to incite
Hopes of some intimate delight
Where many a welcome and a kiss
Would open a new door to bliss.
O, then I shivered and grew hot
And fell in love, poor senseless sot,
From head to foot upon the spot,
Doomed beyond doubt to suffer this
By some fierce vengeful nemesis
Through heaven's will and my own wish
I quivered in her net, poor fish.

    'The legal knot at once was tied,
I was a bridegroom, she a bride.
The folly of a wedding day
Made wits and money flee away
I paid when anyone said pay.
No one can censure that, for by it
I managed to avert a riot,
The men, all vagrants, grew less rough,
The clerk seemed satisfied enough,
The priest (for reasons doubtless good)
Showed the most boundless gratitude.
As quickly in the neighbours ran
We lit the torches, and began
Upon the tables crammed with food
As plentiful as it was good,
And sang and drank and carried on
Sousing and shouting till the dawn.

    'If but my life had gone aright
I should upon my christening night
Have choked upon my baby food,
Before I'd have chosen or thought it good
To marry a wife who would have me where
She'd madden my life and grey my hair
And leave me ruined beyond repair
Without wit or friend and the cupboard bare

Yet young and old brought word to me
Of her reckless generosity,
At tables and inns foods and drinks were free
For married and single, for all but me.
Long had industrious tongues made clear
To everyone my wife was dear.
'Twas longer still till I received
News much too good to be believed,
And every pair that lent an ear
To it would hold their breath in fear
That, if I ever got to hear,
I'd foam off all my clothes and melt,
Off on the wind like Suibhne Geilt.
Nor would I accept what, being blind
I thought was fiction ill-designed
Or joke or ill-aimed stroke unkind,
Until her womb told truly how
'Twas no mere cock and bull tale now.
A real bull had bulled my cow
And made her calve a lot too soon.
To feel so heartless at this boon,
How very tragical a mirth
On that night warm with my child's birth.

    'Fuss, rush and tumult then grew wild
Round ailing wife and swaddled child,
A posset on hot embers laid,
Churn-dashes splashing, butter made
With milk and white bread into pap
Well sugared, which by no mishap
Fell in the greedy midwife's lap.

    'The neighbour women all retire
To hold committee round the fire
Looking at me, till loud and clear
They let their whispers hit my ear:
"Let's give now for the thousandth time
Praise to the lights sublime,
Although this clay's unripened I'm
Able to see, with everyone,
The father imaged in the son.

God save us, Saive, what set of limb,
Look you, the long straight back of him,
He wags his fingers and his toes,
Why those bold little fists can close,
Whoever saw such strength of bone
And all the flesh that he has grown!"
     'They went through this heredity
Tracing each trait straight back through me.
They made my good complexion grace
The perfect oval of his face,
Fine nose and bright brow of my race,
Expression, shape and cut and style,
My cast of eye, my very smile,
They did through every member go
Seeking to make my semblance show
From top of head to tip of toe.
But look or glimpse I could not get,
One breath of wind would kill the pet
– All present said that, in a mind
To keep me ignorant and blind –
"Why one slight draught would liquidate
The creature, it's so delicate."
     'Out then in angry words I spoke
The holy Name did I invoke
Swore to throw greeshugh (in that stroke
By which a fairy changeling's banished)
Words ignorant wrath left badly rhymed
But yet at them resistance vanished,
The old hags found them too well timed
And let me have him to have peace
Smoothed with such soothing words as these:
"Pick him up lightly, and try not to knock him,
See you go easy, don't squeeze him or shock him.
Don't let him get too upset when you rock him,
It's much to be feared he's not long for this earth,
– She got a bad shaking that hastened his birth –
Put him down carefully now on the bed,
He can't last that long but we'll soon see him dead;
Did he breathe on till morning, and the priest to arrive

42

The once he's anointed, he's no right to survive."
'I spread him on my knee and took
The wrappings off for a good look
At a sturdy urchin tight and tough
Ready already to get rough,
His heels kicked hard, he'd a wide pair
Of shoulders, with thick growths of hair
Not only here, but also there,
Strong fists and forearms, lots of bone,
The ears well set, the nails well grown,
Wide nostrils, well developed eyes,
Well sinewed knees to exercise,
One seldom sees a pup like that
Flesh, muscle but with little fat.
'Hear in my cry the whole land call
Pleading with thee the case of all:
Regard with pity not with scorn
All wearers of the cuckold's horn,
And heed the wisdom in them born.
Abolish marriage vows to priests
Let all breed freely as do beasts.
Though green as ever is her hue
Ireland's inhabitants are few,
But without those vain prayers they pray
We'll fill her full of heroes gay.
No need for noisy wedding day,
Liquor in quarts, or band to pay,
No topers who are quiet at first,
Then rowdy when they whet their thirst
God's son made seeds to come to birth
Unaided by all priests on earth.
The seed he gives men leave to sow
Flourishes freely here below
They're mostly vigorous men of parts
With sound and healthy heads and hearts,
Unmarried mothers' sons I find
Are never blemished, bent or blind,
And the legitimate are never
As tall or strong or sharp or clever.

It's easy to bring this to proof
With this one here beneath the roof.
See him lie quiet, why should he blench?
No, bring him over to this bench,
Look at him closely, though so young,
He's a piece of flesh well set and sprung,
With trunk and branches all to suit
Without one fault in hand or foot.
He wasn't born old or too weak to stand, or
A loose bent shape like a goosey gander
With a head too fat to know where to wander,
But a healthy vigorous young tree.
But what sort of father now had he?
'Twas no sickly victim chained for life
To a termagant treadmill of a wife,
'Twas no toneless, boneless, stoneless waster
With no wish for a woman or power to taste her
Who filled with tomcat lust gone mad
Some woman's womb with this fine lad
Whose young limbs' energy and grace
Suffice to prove that in his case
This merry little get was got
Mid healthy sounds when blood was hot.
      'Do not, O starry queen, retain
That useless rule that can't restrain,
Yet ruins myriads by the strain
That strives and tries and sighs in vain.
Arouse the slothful out of slumber,
Throw off the cloaks and chains that cumber,
Put the young churlish seed on stud
To complement old, spent, blue blood.
Give freedom now to nature's force
As rich and poor have intercourse,
Till those of high and low condition
Combine together in coition.
Proclaim again and yet again,
Make it to every region plain,
That young and old are free to fill
All female vessels that they will

With legal semen uncontrolled.
We'll thus bring back the age of gold
And see new wisdom in the Gaels
And glorious vigour in their males
As in the old heroic tales,
Till Goll Mac Mórna re-exists
In all the waists and backs and fists
Of men of this and every nation.
Fertility's regeneration
Shall brightly-lighted skies beget,
Spawn swarms of fish in every net,
And grow too without any toil
Green vegetables in mountain soil,
And men and women for this thing
Shall evermore thy praises sing
And cry, as they together cling,
And to a joyful climax bring.'

The Damsel sat still all that while
Listening to him without one smile,
Then leapt up swiftly when patience broke
When her wrath boiled up and began to smoke,
And her eyes flashed lightning and thus she spoke:
'By Creag Liath's crown of majesty,
But for the pity felt by me
For your unhealthy levity
And ignorant senility,
And my need to keep my dignity
Before this reverent company,
With my sharp nails I'd scrape and tear
Your thick head from your thin neck there,
And dump you like a lump of meat,
Upon this table; how I'd treat
You then I'd better not repeat,
Till I'd thrown your soul with its life-thread drawn
To the roll on the rollers of Acheron.
        'No answer shall you have from me,
We're not amused nor can we be
At minds diseased like yours that must

45

Arouse no feelings but disgust.
Instead the story plain and clear
I'll tell now to their worships here
Of how this lady came to do
What ruined her – and marry you.
She had been enfeebled and met defeat
Without clothes to cover or hearth to heat,
Without kin to love her or friend to greet,
Pushed from the pillar to the post,
Although all hopes in life were lost,
She never stopped by night or day
Earning her bread, and worked away,
Receiving treatment most unfair
From women not as good as her.
     'When all but drowned she thought she saw
Deliverance in this man of straw,
Who promised her a leisured life
If only she would be his wife.
He'd treat her well and not be mean,
She'd be well-dressed and warm and clean,
With cows to milk, a house to keep,
A feather bed and no end of sleep,
Her hearth would never lack a fire,
Whatever turf that might require,
A sod wall and a sturdy roof
Both of them wind and water proof
Would shut off all the draughts that rose,
She'd have wool and flax to spin for clothes.
     'Oh 'twas very well that that serpent knew
And all in the world could see it too
That it was not love or affection drew
Such a pearl among girls to become his wife
She had suffered lack for so long in her life
It was only a longing to have her fill
That ever made her say "I will".
     'A heavy atmosphere of dread
Hung over the night-life she led,
No hopes of pleasure, but instead
Dim misery by fidgets fed

Unpillowing her aching head,
Pushing her body from the bed,
With those old heavy legs of lead
That always seemed to need to spread,
Or she was given a cold shoulder
As hard as ice and even colder,
And feared a further iceberg freeze
Soon to emerge in two sharp knees,
Or that old pair of skinny feet
The fire had singed but could not heat.
Think of that body there beside
Her, old, sick, withered, spent and dried!
Is there lady alive but would fade to grey
To have married a faggot, and have to say
That not twice in a year did he show her a wish
To know was she girl, boy, flesh or fish?
'Twas cruelly hard to do her stretch
Chained to that impotent old wretch
Always so dismal and so grim
Without one stir of life in him.
She needed someone, we may hint
To come twice nightly and imprint
The very devil of a dint
And scutch her as one scutches lint.
    'But you must not think that she was to blame
Or ever proved frigid or dull or tame
Like many a quiet, gentle nun
She could be vivacious and full of fun
– If someone did but appreciate her
As will of course have to happen later.
She would have done her very best
To entertain her every guest
Holding all night without protest
A panting lover to her breast,
Meeting with equal palpitations
The liveliest lancer's liquidations.
She'd have opened to oblige a friend
And welcomed him between her thighs,
And hoped it would not ever end,

47

Flat on her back with close-shut eyes.
She'd welcome every piece of luck
And in no case would she have struck,
Even though disinclined at whiles,
Spat, scratched or bitten – all such styles
She'd leave to felines on the tiles.

(Listen to this interpretation –
Nice girls in such a situation
Find remedies for much frustration
In realms of imagination
If overwhelmed by temptation
Thoughts grow too vividly conjunctive
They're only pluperfect subjunctive,
While happily married people live
With them in the indicative.
She thought such thoughts would be no sin
If only she could bring him in
And so let's go back and begin
Where she relinquishing the styles
She'd leave to felines on the tiles,
Prepares to welcome him with smiles)
She spreads beside him her soft charms
Envelops him with legs and arms
And lies there quietly and warms
Him, but she sometimes to distract
Remorseless thought, is forced to act,
To mouth his mouth her mouth must go,
While fingers exercise below.
Often with one foot round him, she
Rubs him up, down from waist to knee,
With that soft brush of pubic hair
The most cherubic ladies wear,
Or does the quilt and blanket tear
From him, till hip and thigh lay bare,
Poor lass, alas, who does but dream on
Hopes unfulfilled, unboarded beam on
By one whom none of her persuasions
Could force to rise to these occasions,

No use to tickle or to squeeze it,
Or nudge him suddenly and seize it.
With shame my womanhood recites
How that poor girl would pass whole nights
Hugging the poor old fellow that
Was like the mattress, limp and flat
She never knew which one she felt
As there upon the bed she knelt.
Poor nymph, all aching to be satyred
With quaking limbs and teeth that chattered
Tumbling from side to side she lay
And slept no wink till scrake of day –
Oh, it's easy to talk for old lepers like you
Of the women you never have gone into
That subject needs somebody strong and firm
And you are a poor, old boneless worm!
    'If that modest young matron's weight of need
Led to escapades, then her case I'll plead;
Is there fox on the hill, are there fish by the shore,
Are there eagles that sweep up their prey and soar,
Are there hinds that are blithe when the stags get gay
That would go for a year or a single day
Without snatching pasture or catching prey?
There's not one animal or bird
Would be so abjectly absurd;
No hedge no heath no heather they
Will eat, nor do they chew up clay,
When herbs spring up out of the ground
And grass in plenty grows all round.
Dispute, refute that if you can
You poor apology for man!
What lack you as you sit at table
If she all month was hospitable?
And if she did for three months then
Receive some twenty million men,
Need you feel nervous and assume
That you would not find lots of room?
Silly old billy, would you try
To teem or drink the Shannon dry,

Or take a wooden bowl and pour
The whole salt ocean on the shore.
Cut out such folly from your head
And wind a bandage round instead!
Relax and don't go mad to find
A wife so generously inclined,
If she spent the whole day having everyone
She'd have more than enough for you when she'd done.
     'Alas, alack, that jealousy
So bad in you, we're glad to see
In vigorous, sinewy, healthy he-men
Erect, strong-willed, well filled with semen,
In bawdy rowdies who go round
On visit, sport or courtship bound
Lusty endeavourers who ache
To give more than they ever take
Strong men well-armed keep wives content
But you are old and impotent
And cannot stand nor yet present
And all your ammunition's spent ... !
     'My head might well go wholly grey
Wondering through wandering thought away:
The object of my fond research
Is my own old ancestral church,
Why are its clergy women-free
And given to celibacy?
Restrictions I cannot endure,
Bring agonies I cannot cure,
I show great patience through it all
Whereas my anger is but small
We women see what we require,
And what our lonely hearts desire,
And what might mollify our itches
Shut off by those black broadcloth breeches!
A sensitive young maid must be
Reminded of her poverty
And drop her eyelashes to see
Those comely limbs' great grace and power,
Those bright full cheeks with smiles aflower,

That waist, that body we see sway
Those two huge hemispheres away,
That youth, that beauty, pure and gay,
Well marrowboned, and full of flesh.
Straight in the back and stout and fresh
In men so manly without doubt
Desire can never peter out.
They must for learning which they treasure
Have opportunity for leisure
And wealth and means too in due measure
To drink and entertain at pleasure
And sleep upon a feather bed
And be on ham and bacon fed
And drink good wines and eat white bread.
They are usually obvious
And young and strong and numerous,
And our experience can tell
That they are flesh and blood as well.
  'Some I'd spare gladly, who'd require
Castrati from the papal choir,
Insects whose business is to ail
Colts that know only how to stale.
But how can those whose manliest part
Could drive a nail straight in with art
Go idling off in dreams to Roam
With so much work to do at home?
Some feel repentant, we'll retrieve
Them yet, I verily believe;
With them, on their return to grace,
Severity were out of place.
It were unfair in one's excitement
To damn by general indictment,
Order the order's head to fall,
Arrest, condemn and hang them all.
All them to death I'd hate to do
Or drown for one the whole ship's crew!
Some always have been scoundrels. True.
Others have never had a clue;
Dull, cruel, hard and avaricious,

The coldest, hatefullest, most vicious
Of all is the misogynist
Whose mother once made him exist.
All such as those will not be missed.
   'But a good number could not be
More full of love and charity,
Flowing with generosity.
Churns, cows and cornstacks often show
The little blessings which they sow
As often as they on visitation
Relieve someone of her temptation.
I've often heard them praised, none mocks
All such true fathers of their flocks
Who wisely plan and swiftly act
With wisdom and unerring tact.
Men whisper of them near at hand
And rumours too go through the land
I've seen good fruit too from their games
In children bearing borrowed names.
But, O my heart's wings beat their cage
To see them waste their healthiest stage
On women well past middle age
With barren wombs and breasts gone dry.
The lovely ladies are passed by
The country suffers from the strain
Young beauty's treated with disdain
The holy seed is spent in vain.
   'The isle of saints lies waste indeed
All through this waste of saintly seed
Which foolish laws forbid to breed.
I leave it for you to disclose,
True nut of Wisdom, diagnose
The root cause of the clergy's woes.
To lie in lonely beds awake
I think a ruinous mistake
But I am without sight and blind,
Enlighten my poor ignorant mind!
Remind us of that living word
Still in your memory, you've heard

52

What prophets and apostles said
Sent by the King to rouse the dead:
Say what authority induced
Such celibacy mass-produced?
Who had authority to tell
The natural feelings not to swell
But starve and sicken as they dwell
Imprisoned in this dungeon fell?
Paul never told one man he must
Not marry, but forbade all lust;
Give up your kin and family
However great your love may be
Cleave henceforth solely to your wife
One with her for the rest of life.
My female efforts are but vain
To sum up what the law makes plain
Before a judge as great as you,
Who'll yet agree that it's all true.
Pearl, to whose perfect memory
The great event's contemporary,
The history a mystery of light,
The heavenly vision present sight,
Set the eternal music free,
Declare the words of victory.
O, let the Lamb damn lies and say
Out truth that shall not pass away;
It was no spinster made God human,
God's Mother was a married woman
He through his prophets rules the good
Of highly favoured womanhood.
        'Hear now, O Faery Queene, my cry,
Sibyl sent hither from the sky,
Scion of celestial royalty,
To stoop to lift what is cast down
Adds brighter glories to thy crown,
Hear my appeal without a frown.
        'Consider what things make today
Many young ladies pine away,
Think of the thousand female needs,

The nubile spinsters no man heeds,
Think of the young girls in their teens
Swarming like goslings on the greens,
Think of the tots that swing a skirt,
Black faced, they dabble in the dirt,
They seldom laugh, they often cry,
They're not attractive to the eye.
Yet they have appetites to eat
All substances both sour and sweet,
Whatever they can get eat they,
Green vegetables, curds and whey,
And then they shoot up suddenly
Into the age of puberty,
Grow hairs and bosoms, come to be
Oozing with femininity.
    'O my heart's pain! My vain desire
Must advertise what I require
In letters of electric fire:
But I have but little hope or none
And husbands now are hardly won
When women in Munster are three to one!
Those western regions are in fact
So needy, they're too weak to act,
The situation's desperate,
Our leaders all procrastinate,
Ireland, emptied; and in decay
Waves with rank crops of weed today,
Even the young are bent and grey.
    'O, show intolerance to see
Unmarried women such as me!
Let the mean men that stay unmated
Be in this land not tolerated,
Find me a husband speedily
Of whatsoever sort he be!
Saddle and bit, well housetrained they
Will learn in due time to obey
Parcel them up, and we'll attend
From that on to the latter end.'
    The lovely lady leapt up on

54

The bench, and like a ray of sun-
Light round the hall her splendour shone.
Her figure and face were young and fair
And her voice rang loud and set hearts astir.
'Silence,' a bailiff cried, 'in Court,'
And did with it her fists contort.
Her mouth poured out enlightenment
(To hear which every ear was bent):
'Poor maid, so often disappointed,
Your maiden speech was so well pointed
That my approval has been won
What you have said shall now be done.
I see, as see, alas, I must
That all those daughters of disgust
That come of Orla, Mór and Maeve,
Mean creatures, and by no means brave
Whether they spend, or scrape and save
The proletarian lumps from Lee
The stolid Dublin bourgeoisie,
Safe pussies, sly manoeuvrers,
Are hoping now to catch in snares
Some son of the old nobility,
Someone at least with a degree.
      'So we enact now and decree
That women are henceforward free
To take and towrope by the head
All over twenty not yet wed
And to tie each to meet his doom
To this tree here beside the tomb,
Tear off his coat and vest then, crack
The rope's end, flay his waist and back!
From them you then may choose a mate
Whereas we'll have to liquidate
Those older bachelors, grown stale
Who never did a woman nail,
They've let their manly passions fail
And what in them might have amused
Someone, is withered and disused,
They'd never take those they could get,

They'd denigrate each maid they met
And praise another for a peach
Up on some high branch out of reach –
So do just as you wish with each.

    'Be ye ingenious inventors,
Lustfully industrious tormentors,
Ye women, dimmed by dark desires,
Contrive, to sate your frustrate fires,
Stings from great redhot rusty nails,
Kindle whinbushes under tails,
Each woman, when she has a mind
Is very cleverly unkind,
Consult together how your scorn
May make men wish themselves unborn.
I grant the necessary powers,
Start now, and let it last for hours.
Let us see agonies and groans
Before you kill the spent old drones.

    'But what I've said will not apply
To married men when they go dry,
Some limp and loose no longer can
Even if they wished to, play the man,
Others, more rigidly intense
Can take, not give, the joys of sense,
Their barren semen or albumen
Can never fertilise a woman.
Let them retire and act as covers
While a full stud of hot young lovers
Fill to the brim with youthful life
The much rejuvenated wife.
(What visions fill the imagination
With things beyond all expectation
That fit now into speculation
Unlimited experimentation
Voluptuous sex-education
By reproductive recreation
Rejuvenation of the wife
Filled to the brim with youthful life
Through natural insemination

Of a planned future generation
A pointer and a pilot station
Towards final eugenification)!
Give me consistent cuckoldry
Such as even now I often see
Practised in ways approved by me;
Wiry old fellows foolishly
Worn out with housework night and day
Skilful wife-pleasers who obey
Them, cherish them in every way,
And, having still for them a kindness,
Their good repute they in their blindness
Keep sheltered from all shame and slander
While the wives safely polyander
The husband's part is nominal
They are the name by which to call
The children ... and that is all.
Arrangements which I'm satisfied
You couldn't better if you tried
I've more to say before we scatter
(Much as I hate females that chatter).
I hear breathed one top-secret matter:
Speak quietly, let your words be few,
Don't form, much less express a view,
Be silent if you can't agree,
Don't contradict the hierarchy.
Leave them, since they're so sensitive,
In that long past age in which they live.
Yet married men they yet shall be
Whoever lives long enough to see.
The day shall come when plenary
Conciliar authority
Empowered by the Papacy,
Appointing a select Commission
To look into this land's condition,
Shall give you healthy constitutions
All tied up well in resolutions
And throw back to you with a thud
From its long fallow that lost stud

So sound, sound flesh go wild O blood
Let red hot pokers go on duty
To soothe the soft desires of beauty!
    'No other single mother's son
(I write, read, let me see you run)
Will I have in my baliwick,
All such male spinsters make me sick,
Grey, weedy creatures, take a stick
And chase them out of Erin quick.
    'But I must leave you now to go
Upon a circuit long and slow
Since this all-Munster visitation
Will not permit procrastination
Most cases being as yet unheard.
    'Once back then – let men hear my word
And tremble if they've cause for fear –
I'll make short work, when I appear
With every bachelor found here.
    'Some, thinking with minds cruel and base
To find distinction in disgrace,
Drop names of ladies whom they woo,
The public get a private view
Of everything they say and do.
They find it pleasant to act thus,
They even term it chivalrous.
Even she who has denied a favour
Will find denials cannot save her.
They've thus corrupted and betrayed
Many a chaste matron and young maid.
Yet it was not concupiscence
That was the cause of their offence
Or heat of blood, or lust intense
Or pleasure in the joys of sense
Or a priapism too immense –
They want a noisy audience
That roars and gloats and licks and chaps:
They well deserve to get the claps.
    'At some no women set their caps,
Many have never felt at all

The pleasure of their sex's call,
Their manliness is just a loud
And empty boast before a crowd,
Incapable of any action
Which is to women's satisfaction.
Destructive female rage must follow
Abolishing deceits so hollow.
    'That I'll let them anticipate.
You're in hurry and can't wait
I'll take your case upon the spot,
So strike now while the iron's hot.
And I'll come back next month I vow
To break those others to the plough.'
    I kept my spellbound eyes upon
That starry queen till she had done.
My heart sank as she ceased to speak
My wits grew sick, my bones grew weak,
A hideous madness came to seize me
A deadly palsy came to freeze me,
And all the land began to quake
And all the hall with it to shake,
And all the while her ringing words
Danced in my ears like singing birds.
    I see the bouncing Bailiff come
I change my colour as her thumb
And fingers close like pinchers, wrench
Me by the ear up towards the Bench.
    That babe that hated spinsterhood
Clenched her two fists as there she stood
Like one who's on to something good,
And then she jumped her own full height,
Crying, in rapturous delight:
'I've got the object of my lust,
How long I've longed, you stale old crust,
To have that seat of yours to dust.
Mean-hearted thing without affections
Defying warnings and corrections
Unlicensed still in your defection,
I'm in the Van of your detection,

The day has come for you to be
A member of the helotry
Subjected to the matriarchy.
You useless slob, make no pretence
To try to put up a defence.
What woman witness will advance
Full proof of work as a free lance?
What good have you done in your life?
Produce, consoled, one lonely wife.

   'With your permission I present
Him, Maiden Ma'am most reverent,
For medical examination.
Strip quick ... let's start the operation.
Look at his body, see each limb,
No blemish can we find in him
Which he can plead as an excuse
For not being of female use.
Examine him from head to feet,
He doesn't look exactly sweet,
Yet head and members, all complete,
Make this ill-favoured animal
Quite fit for mating after all.
He shakes his top there like a tree!
He'd wriggle out of it would he?
Let me see him tied up for life,
He can't say "No" now to a wife!
He's palely puffy for a man –
– I for my part prefer suntan –
I with men's bones and vertebrae
Would not find fault in any way
Men humped or hollow-backed yet can
Stand up erect and play the man.
Bow legs can swiftly strike a blow
And buckle knees much vigour show.

   'He isn't married yet we see,
Owing to some foul deformity
He hides with such dexterity
See how the sour bap girns at me –
Which still, 'twould seem, has left him free

To enter high society,
A music-maker and disporter,
He's popular in every quarter,
Wherever company is gay
He will be there to drink and play
With cultured men of education,
But I won't give him an ovation,
And all his friends are men of worth,
Gentle and generous from birth.
If I had him in my house
How I'd tame and housetrain the Louse.
In spite of poise and *dignity*
He's as *charming* as a man can be
His *profitable quality*
Shall benefit posterity
And a *lively intellect* proclaim
Him *Merry* man in *air* and *name!*
    'The Lord who did this earth create
Ordained all animals should mate
Yet you, you beast, keep celibate,
You'll soon go grey it's gone so late.
I thrill to see you feel the knout –
No, don't you try to talk it out.
You're labelled felon beyond doubt,
With all adult unmarried men
Of years exceeding three times ten.
You, to whom Patience gives a name,
Hear me, and grant the help I claim.
A spinster, leaping from the shelf,
A useless piece of dusty delf,
I'm sharp-edged to avenge myself,
And call on each avenging maid –
Dear women, lend your sex's aid,
Come let me see the debt well paid!
Come, help me to arrest this man,
A rope as quickly as you can
Please Una; see now how she ran.
O dear, why do you hang back Ann?
Bind his two hands behind his back

Máire, don't let the rope go slack.
Muirinn and Maeve have joined the pack
Sheila and Saive are in the claque,
Let now those four the rope's end crack,
Come carry out with many a whack
The penalty our Queen prescribes,
Let every cord cut separate kibes,
Let the big, pink pig squeal afresh
Each time they sink deep in his flesh
Lavish all torments you can find
And don't spare Brian's bare behind.
Lift the hand high let the scourge whirr
Make an example of him there,
And then, dear ladies, sit and purr!
But first cut deep, pay all we owe,
Take off his skin from head to toe
Round Ireland let the echoes go,
That all the bachelors that hear
May feel their hearts beat faint with fear.
    'This is, and will ever be,
I think, a wise and just decree.
It's right now to inscribe the date
I'll tell you how to calculate
A thousand first before he lies –
Coax, steal, embezzle, terrorise
From it one hundred and ten,
And double the remainder then,
One week precisely from the birth
Of the one Son of heaven and earth.'

The girl takes up the pen; my head
Is one wild whirl of fear and dread
To think, once they have done that, they
Will take me first to scourge and flay;
Slow she writes the long date. The Guard
Sit and watch me, their eyes are hard;
    The torment ends, the storm clouds break
    I rub my eyes, I jump awake!

Brian Merriman – Translated by Cosslett Ó Cuinn

The Wild Old Wicked Man

'Because I am mad about women
I am mad about the hills,'
Said that wild old wicked man
Who travels where God wills.
'Not to die on the straw at home,
Those hands to close these eyes,
That is all I ask, my dear,
From the old man in the skies.
          Daybreak and a candle-end.

'Kind are all your words, my dear,
Do not the rest withhold.
Who can know the year, my dear,
When an old man's blood grows cold?
I have what no young man can have
Because he loves too much.
Words I have that can pierce the heart,
But what can he do but touch?'
          Daybreak and a candle-end.

Then said she to that wild old man,
His stout stick under his hand,
'Love to give or to withhold
Is not at my command.
I gave it all to an older man:
That old man in the skies.
Hands that are busy with His beads
Can never close those eyes.'
          Daybreak and a candle-end.

'Go your ways, O go your ways,
I choose another mark,
Girls down on the seashore
Who understand the dark;
Bawdy talk for the fishermen;

63

A dance for the fisher-lads;
When dark hangs upon the water
They turn down their beds.
Daybreak and a candle-end.

'A young man in the dark am I,
But a wild old man in the light,
That can make a cat laugh, or
Can touch by mother wit
Things hid in their marrow-bones
From time long passed away,
Hid from all those warty lads
That by their bodies lay.
Daybreak and a candle-end.

'All men live in suffering,
I know as few can know,
Whether they take the upper road
Or stay content on the low,
Rower bent in his row-boat
Or weaver bent on his loom,
Horseman erect upon horseback
Or child hid in the womb.
Daybreak and a candle-end.

'That some stream of lightning
From the old man in the skies
Can burn out that suffering
No right-taught man denies.
But a coarse old man am I,
I choose the second-best,
I forget it all awhile
Upon a woman's breast.'
Daybreak and a candle-end.

W B Yeats

The Curse

To a sister of an enemy of the author who disapproved of The Playboy.

Lord, confound this surly sister,
Blight her brow with blotch and blister,
Cramp her larynx, lung and liver,
In her guts a galling give her.
Let her live to earn her dinners
In Mountjoy with seedy sinners:
Lord, this judgment quickly bring,
And I'm your servant, J M Synge.

J M Synge

Queens

Seven dog-days we let pass
Naming queens in Glenmacnass,
All the rare and royal names
Wormy sheepskin yet retains,
Etain, Helen, Maeve, and Fand,
Golden Deirdre's tender hand,
Bert, the big-foot, sung by Villon,
Cassandra, Ronsard found in Lyon.
Queens of Sheba, Meath and Connaught,
Coifed with crown, or gaudy bonnet,
Queens whose finger once did stir men,
Queens were eaten of fleas and vermin,
Queens men drew like Monna Lisa,
Or slew with drugs in Rome and Pisa,
We named Lucrezia Crivelli,
And Titian's lady with amber belly,
Queens acquainted in learned sin,
Jane of Jewry's slender shin:
Queens who cut the bogs of Glanna,
Judith of Scripture, and Gloriana,
Queens who wasted the East by proxy,

Or drove the ass-cart, a tinker's doxy,
Yet these are rotten – I ask their pardon –
And we've the sun on rock and garden,
These are rotten, so you're the queen
Of all are living, or have been.

J M Synge

The Journey
(For Elizabeth Ryle)

*Immediately cries were heard. These were the loud wailing of infant souls
weeping at the very entrance-way; never had they had their share of life's
sweetness for the dark day had stolen them from their mother's breasts
and plunged them to their death before their time.*
Virgil, *The Aeneid*, Book VI

And then the dark fell and 'there has never'
I said, 'been a poem to an antibiotic:
never a word to compare with the odes on
the flower of the raw sloe for fever

'or the devious Africa-seeking tern
or the protein treasures of the sea-bed.
Depend on it, somewhere a poet is wasting
his sweet uncluttered metres on the obvious

'emblem instead of the real thing.
Instead of sulpha we shall have hyssop dipped
in the wild blood of the unblemished lamb,
so every day the language gets less

'for the task and we are less with the language.'
I finished speaking and the anger faded
and dark fell and the book beside me
lay open at the page Aphrodite

comforts Sappho in her love's duress.
The poplars shifted their music in the garden,
a child startled in a dream,

my room was a mess –

the usual hardcovers, half-finished cups,
clothes piled up on an old chair –
and I was listening out but in my head was
a loosening and sweetening heaviness,

not sleep, but nearly sleep, not dreaming really
but as ready to believe and still
unfevered, calm and unsurprised
when she came and stood beside me

and I would have known her anywhere
and I would have gone with her anywhere
and she came wordlessly
and without a word I went with her

down down down without so much as
ever touching down but always, always
with a sense of mulch beneath us,
the way of stairs winding down to a river

and as we went on the light went on
failing and I looked sideways to be certain
it was she, misshapen, musical –
Sappho – the scholiast's nightingale

and down we went, again down
until we came to a sudden rest
beside a river in what seemed to be
an oppressive suburb of the dawn.

My eyes got slowly used to the bad light.
At first I saw shadows, only shadows.
Then I could make out women and children
and, in the way they were, the grace of love.

'Cholera, typhus, croup, diphtheria,'
she said, 'in those days they racketed
in every backstreet and alley of old Europe.

Behold the children of the plague'.

Then to my horror I could see to each
nipple some had clipped a limpet shape –
suckling darknesses – while others had their arms
weighed down, making terrible pietàs.

She took my sleeve and said to me, 'be careful.
Do not define these women by their work:
not as washerwomen trussed in dust and sweating,
muscling water into linen by the river's edge

'nor as court ladies brailled in silk
on wool and woven with an ivory unicorn
and hung, nor as laundresses tossing cotton,
brisking daylight with lavender and gossip.

'But these are women who went out like you
when dusk became a dark sweet with leaves,
recovering the day, stooping, picking up
teddy bears and rag dolls and tricycles and buckets –

'love's archaeology – and they too like you
stood boot deep in flowers once in summer
or saw winter come in with a single magpie
in a caul of haws, a solo harlequin.'

I stood fixed. I could not reach or speak to them.
Between us was the melancholy river,
the dream water, the narcotic crossing
and they had passed over it, its cold persuasions.

I whispered, 'let me be
let me at least be their witness,' but she said
'what you have seen is beyond your speech,
beyond song, only not beyond love;

'remember it, you will remember it,'
and I heard her say but she was fading fast
as we emerged under the stars of heaven,

'there are not many of us; you are dear

'and stand beside me as my own daughter.
I have brought you here so you will know forever
the silences in which are our beginnings,
in which we have an origin like water,'

and the wind shifted and the window clasp
opened, banged and I woke up to find
my poetry books stacked higgledy piggledy,
my skirt spread out where I had laid it –

nothing was changed; nothing was more clear
but it was wet and the year was late.
The rain was grief in arrears; my children
slept the last dark out safely and I wept.

Eavan Boland

Envoi

It is Easter in the suburb. Clematis
shrubs the eaves and trellises with pastel.
The evenings lengthen and before the rain
the Dublin mountains become visible.

My muse must be better than those of men
who made theirs in the image of their myth.
The work is half-finished and I have nothing
but the crudest measures to complete it with.

Under the street-lamps the dustbins brighten.
The winter flowering jasmine casts a shadow
outside my window in my neighbour's garden.
These are the things that my muse must know.

She must come to me. Let her come
to be among the donnée, the given.

I need her to remain with me until
the day is over and the song is proven.

Surely she comes, surely she comes to me –
no lizard skin, no paps, no podded womb
about her but a brightening and
the consequences of an April tomb.

What I have done I have done alone.
What I have seen is unverified.
I have the truth and I need the faith.
It is time I put my hand in her side.

If she will not bless the ordinary,
if she will not sanctify the common,
then here I am and here I stay and then am I
the most miserable of women.

Eavan Boland

Fair and Forty

'I may not be visually aware, like I said before
I can't really appreciate art, but even if I did –
Do you think it worth while that Gauguin left
His wife and children just to be self-indulgent
And paint? People tell me the paintings are great,
Why yes, that's an interesting point about
Drunken husbands and wife-beating people who,
After all, do nothing except indulge themselves.
No, your first duty is not to yourself,
And as for talents, why quote the Bible?
Competitiveness is not to be encouraged, after all,
It is as if you are exploiting others. You said,
What about scholarship, well of course, it's exploiting
Others, I can't really explain it, it's anthropological
Pillage. I know a charwoman, who thinks of her
Native land just like Bracque thought about paint,

Well, of course, in her case it's not exploitation
She just feels the distance and imposes an image on it
Equal to anything in modern art – a whole
   fragmentation.
Well, what if Gauguin didn't paint, lots of people,
I suppose, they tell me, would be deprived of pleasure.
What's that in the sum totality of the misery
Of the human race, and yes, his wife was miserable.'

                                  Rosemarie Rowley

Dear Dark Head

Put your head, darling, darling, darling,
Your darling black head my heart above;
Oh, mouth of honey, with the thyme for fragrance,
Who, with heart in breast, could deny you love?
Oh, many and many a young girl for me is pining,
Letting her locks of gold to the cold wind free,
For me, the foremost of our gay young fellows;
But I'd leave a hundred, pure love, for thee!
Then put your head, darling, darling, darling,
Your darling black head my heart above;
Oh, mouth of honey, with the thyme for fragrance,
Who, with heart in breast, could deny you love?

                Anonymous – Translated by Samuel Ferguson

Dicey Reilly

Ah poor old Dicey Reilly, she has taken to the sup,
And poor old Dicey Reilly she will never give it up,
It's off each morning to the pop then she goes in for another
       little drop,
But the heart of the rowl is Dicey Reilly.

She will walk along Fitzgibbon Street with an independent
      air
And then it's down by Summerhill, and as the people stare
She'll say, 'It's nearly half past one, time I went in for
      another little one.'
But the heart of the rowl is Dicey Reilly.

Now at two, pubs close and out she goes as happy as a lark
She'll find a bench to sleep it off down in St Patrick's Park.
She'll wake at five feeling in the pink and say "Tis time for
      another drink.'
But the heart of the rowl is Dicey Reilly.

Now she'll travel far to a dockside bar to have another
      round
And after one or two or three she doesn't feel quite sound
And after four she's a bit unstable, after five underneath the
      table
The heart of the rowl is Dicey Reilly.

Oh they carry her home at twelve o'clock as they do every
      night
Bring her inside, put her on the bed and then turn out the
      light.
Next morning she'll get out of bed and look for a curer for
      her head
But the heart of the rowl is Dicey Reilly.

Ah poor oul Dicey Reilly she has taken to the sup
And poor oul Dicey Reilly she will never give it up.
It's off each morning to the pop then she goes in for another
      little drop
But the heart of the rowl is Dicey Reilly.

Anonymous

Donall Oge

O Donall Oge, if you go across the sea,

Bring myself with you and do not forget it;
And you will have a sweetheart for fair days and market
      days,
And the daughter of the King of Greece beside you at night.

It is late last night the dog was speaking of you;
The snipe was speaking of you in her deep marsh.
It is you are the lonely bird through the woods;
And that you may be without a mate until you find me.

You promised me, and you said a lie to me,
That you would be before me where the sheep are flocked;
I gave a whistle and three hundred cries to you,
And I found nothing there but a bleating lamb.

You promised me a thing that was hard for you,
A ship of gold under a silver mast;
Twelve towns with a market in all of them,
And a fine white court by the side of the sea.

You promised me a thing that is not possible,
That you would give me gloves of the skin of a fish;
That you would give me shoes of the skin of a bird;
And a suit of the dearest silk in Ireland.

O Donall Oge, it is I would be better to you
Than a high, proud, spendthrift lady:
I would milk the cow; I would bring help to you;
And if you were hard pressed, I would strike a blow for you.

O, ochone, and it's not with hunger
Or with wanting food, or drink, or sleep,
That I am growing thin, and my life is shortened;
But it is the love of a young man has withered me away.

It is early in the morning that I saw him coming,
Going along the road on the back of a horse;
He did not come to me; he made nothing of me;
And it is on my way home that I cried my fill.

When I go by myself to the Well of Loneliness,
I sit down and I go through my trouble;
When I see the world and do not see my boy,
He that has an amber shade in his hair.

It was on that Sunday I gave my love to you;
The Sunday that is last before Easter Sunday.
And myself on my knees reading the Passion;
And my two eyes giving love to you for ever.

O, aya! my mother, give myself to him;
And give him all that you have in the world;
Get out yourself to ask for alms,
And do not come back and forward looking for me.

My mother said to me not to be talking with you today,
Or tomorrow, or on Sunday;
It was a bad time she took for telling me that;
It was shutting the door after the house was robbed.

My heart is as black as the blackness of the sloe,
Or as the black coal that is on the smith's forge;
Or as the sole of a shoe left in white halls;
It was you put that darkness over my life.

You have taken the east from me; you have taken the west
         from me
You have taken what is before me and what is behind me;
You have taken the moon, you have taken the sun from me,
And my fear is great that you have taken God from me!

Anonymous – Translated by Lady Gregory

Lapis Lazuli
(For Harry Clifton)

I have heard that hysterical women say
They are sick of the palette and fiddle-bow,
Of poets that are always gay,

74

For everybody knows or else should know
That if nothing drastic is done
Aeroplane and Zeppelin will come out,
Pitch like King Billy bomb-balls in
Until the town lie beaten flat.

All perform their tragic play,
There struts Hamlet, there is Lear,
That's Ophelia, that Cordelia;
Yet they, should the last scene be there,
The great stage curtain about to drop,
If worthy their prominent part in the play,
Do not break up their lines to weep.
They know that Hamlet and Lear are gay;
Gaiety transfiguring all that dread.
All men have aimed at, found and lost;
Black out; Heaven blazing into the head:
Tragedy wrought to its uttermost.
Though Hamlet rambles and Lear rages,
And all the drop-scenes drop at once
Upon a hundred thousand stages,
It cannot grow by an inch or an ounce.

On their own feet they came, or on shipboard,
Camel-back, horse-back, ass-back, mule-back,
Old civilisations put to the sword.
Then they and their wisdom went to rack:
No handiwork of Callimachus,
Who handled marble as if it were bronze,
Made draperies that seemed to rise
When sea-wind swept the corner, stands;
His long lamp-chimney shaped like the stem
Of a slender palm, stood but a day;
All things fall and are built again,
And those that build them again are gay.

Two Chinamen, behind them a third,
Are carved in lapis lazuli,
Over them flies a long-legged bird,

A symbol of longevity;
The third, doubtless a serving-man,
Carries a musical instrument.

Every discoloration of the stone,
Every accidental crack or dent,
Seems a water-course or an avalanche,
Or lofty slope where it still snows
Though doubtless plum or cherry-branch
Sweetens the little half-way house
Those Chinamen climb towards, and I
Delight to imagine them seated there;
There, on the mountain and the sky,
On all the tragic scene they stare.
One asks for mournful melodies;
Accomplished fingers begin to play.
Their eyes mid many wrinkles, their eyes,
Their ancient, glittering eyes, are gay.

W B Yeats

The Ballad of William Bloat

In a mean abode, on the Shankill Road,
Lived a man called William Bloat,
He had a wife, the curse of his life,
Who continually got his goat.
So, one day at dawn, with her nightdress on,
He cut her bloody throat.

With a razor-gash, he settled her hash,
O never was crime so quick;
But the steady drip, on the pillow-slip,
Of her life-blood made him sick,
And the pool of gore on the bedroom floor,
Grew clotted, cold and thick.

And yet he was glad that he'd done what he had,

When she lay there stiff and still;
But a sudden awe of the angry law
Struck his soul with an icy chill.
So to finish the fun so well begun
He resolved himself to kill.

Then he took the sheet off his wife's cold feet,
And he twisted it into a rope,
And he hanged himself from the pantry shelf –
'Twas an easy end, let's hope –
In the face of death, with his latest breath,
He solemnly cursed the Pope.

But the strangest turn to the whole concern
Is only just beginnin'!
He went to hell, but his wife got well,
And she's still alive and sinnin',
For the razor blade was German made,
But the sheet was Irish linen!

Raymond Calvert

Biddy Mulligan
The Pride of the Coombe

I'm a buxom fine widow, I live in a spot,
In Dublin they call it the Coombe;
My shops and my stalls are laid out on the street,
And my palace consists of one room.
I sell apples and oranges, nuts and split peas,
Bananas and sugar-stick sweet,
On Saturday night I sell secondhand clothes
From the floor of my stall on the street.

Chorus
You may travel from Clare
To the County Kildare,
From Francis Street on to Macroom,
But where would you see

A fine widow like me?
Biddy Mulligan, the pride of the Coombe.

I sell fish on a Friday, spread out on a board
The finest you'd find in the sae,
But the best is my herrings, fine Dublin Bay herrings,
There's herrings for dinner today.
I have a son Mick, and he's great on the flute
He plays in the Longford Street Band,
It would do your heart good to see him march out,
On a Sunday for Dollymount strand.

Chorus

In the Park on a Sunday, I make quite a dash,
The neighbours look on with surprise,
With my Aberdeen shawlie thrown over my head,
I dazzle the sight of their eyes.
At Patrick Street corner for sixty-four years,
I've stood and no one can deny,
That while I stood there, no person could dare
To say black was the white of my eye.

Chorus

Seamus Kavanagh

The Yellow Bittern

The yellow bittern that never broke out
In a drinking-bout, might as well have drunk;
His bones are thrown on a naked stone
Where he lived alone like a hermit monk.
O yellow bittern! I pity your lot,
Though they say that a sot like myself is curst –
I was sober a while, but I'll drink and be wise
For fear I should die in the end of thirst.

It's not for the common birds that I'd mourn,
The blackbird, the corncrake or the crane,
But for the bittern that's shy and apart
And drinks in the marsh from the lone bog-drain.
Oh! if I had known you were near your death,
While my breath held out I'd have run to you,
Till a splash from the Lake of the Son of the Bird
Your soul would have stirred and waked anew.

My darling told me to drink no more
Or my life would be o'er in a little short while;
But I told her 'tis drink gives me health and strength,
And will lengthen my road for many a mile.
You see how the bird of the long smooth neck,
Could get his death from the thirst at last –
Come, son of my soul, and drain your cup,
You'll get no sup when your life is past.

In a wintering island by Constantine's halls,
A bittern calls from a wineless place,
And tells me that hither he cannot come
Till the summer is here and the sunny days.
When he crosses the stream there and wings o'er the sea,
Then a fear comes to me he may fail in his flight –
Well, the milk and the ale are drunk every drop,
And a dram won't stop our thirst this night.

Cathal Buidhe Mac Elgun (c1750) – Translated by Thomas MacDonagh

Bold Phelim Brady, The Bard of Armagh

Oh! List to the lay of a poor Irish harper,
And scorn not the strains of his old withered hand,
But remember those fingers they could once move sharper
To raise the merry strains of his dear native land;
It was long before the shamrock our green isle's loved

emblem
Was crushed in its beauty 'neath the Saxon lion's paw
I was called by the colleens of the village and valley
Bold Phelim Brady, the Bard of Armagh.

How I long for to muse on the days of my boyhood,
Though four score and three years have flitted since then,
Still it gives sweet reflections, as every young joy should,
That merry-hearted boys make the best of old men.
At a pattern or fair I could twist my shillela
Or trip through a jig with my brogues bound with straw,
Whilst all the pretty maidens around me assembled
Loved bold Phelim Brady, the Bard of Armagh.

Although I have travelled this wide world over,
Yet Erin's my home and my parent to me,
Then oh, let the ground that my old bones shall cover
Be cut from the soil that is trod by the free.
And when sergeant death in his cold arms shall embrace me,
O lull me to sleep with sweet Erin go bragh,
By the side of my Kathleen, my young wife, O place me,
Then forget Phelim Brady, the Bard of Armagh.

Anonymous

The Boyne Water
(This is the oldest version of the famous Orange song)

July the First, of a morning clear, one thousand six hundred
     and ninety,
King William did his men prepare, of thousands he had
     thirty;
To fight King James and all his foes, encamped near the
     Boyne Water,
He little fear'd, though two to one, their multitudes to
     scatter.

King William called his officers saying: 'Gentlemen, mind
     your station,

And let your valour here be shown before this Irish nation;
My brazen walls let no man break, and your subtle foes
       you'll scatter,
Be sure you show them good English play as you go over the
       water.'

Both foot and horse they marched on, intending them to
       batter,
But the brave Duke Schomberg he was shot as he crossed
       over the water.
When that King William did observe the brave Duke Schom-
       berg falling,
He rein'd his horse with a heavy heart, on the Enniskilleners
       calling:

'What will you do for me, brave boys – see yonder men re-
       treating?
Our enemies encourag'd are and English drums are beating;'
He says, 'My boys, feel no dismay at the losing of one com-
       mander,
For God shall be our King this day, and I'll be general
       under.'

Within four yards of our fore-front, before a shot was fired,
A sudden snuff they got that day, which little they desired;
For horse and man fell to the ground, and some hung in
       their saddle:
Others turn'd up their forked ends, which we call 'coup de
       ladle'.

Prince Eugene's regiment was the next, on our right hand
       advanced,
Into a field of standing wheat, where Irish horses pranced –
But the brandy ran so in their heads, their senses all did
       scatter,
They little thought to leave their bones that day at the Boyne
       Water.

Both men and horse lay on the ground, and many lay there

bleeding:
I saw no sickles there that day – but, sure, there was sharp
    shearing.

Now, praise God, all true Protestants, and heaven's and
    earth's Creator,
For the deliverance that He sent our enemies to scatter.
The Church's foes will pine away, like churlish-hearted
    Nabal,
For our deliverer came this day like the great Zorobabel.

So praise God, all true Protestants, and I will say no further,
But had the Papists gain'd the day there would have been
    open murder.
Although King James and many more were ne'er that way
    inclined,
It was not in their power to stop what the rabble they de-
    signed.

Anonymous

The Wearin' o' the Green

O Paddy dear, an' did you hear the news that's goin' round?
The shamrock is by law forbid to grow on Irish ground!
No more Saint Patrick's day we'll keep, his colour can't be
    seen,
For there's a cruel law agin' the wearin' o' the Green!
I met wid Napper Tandy, and he took me by the hand,
And he said, 'How's poor ould Ireland, and how does she
    stand?'
She's the most disthressful country that iver yet was seen,
For they're hangin' men and women for the wearin' o' the
    Green.

And if the colour we must wear is England's cruel Red,
Let it remind us of the blood that Ireland has shed;
Then pull the shamrock from your hat, and throw it on the

sod,

And never fear, 'twill take root there, tho' under foot 'tis
       trod!

When law can stop the blades of grass from growin' as they
       grow,

And when the leaves in summer-time their colour dare not
       show,

Then I will change the colour, too, I wear in my caubeen,

But till that day, plase God, I'll stick to wearin' o' the Green.

Anonymous

The above represents the anonymous, street version of the song dating from 1798. It was slightly altered by Dion Boucicault (1822-1890) who added a third stanza in his published version:

But if at last our colour should be torn from Ireland's heart,

Her sons with shame and sorrow from the dear old isle will
       part;

I've heard a whisper of a country that lies beyond the sea,

Where rich and poor stand equal in the light of freedom's
       day.

O Erin, must we leave you, driven by a tyrant's hand?

Must we ask a mother's blessing from a strange and distant
       land?

Where the cruel cross of England shall nevermore be seen

And where, please God, we'll live and die still wearin' o' the
       Green.

Croppies Lie Down

We soldiers of Erin, so proud of the name,
Will raise upon Rebels and Frenchmen our fame;
We'll fight to the last in the honest old cause,
And guard our religion, our freedom, and laws;
We'll fight for our country, our king, and his crown,
And make all the traitors and croppies lie down.

Down, down, croppies lie down.

The rebels so bold – when they've none to oppose –
To houses and hay-stacks are terrible foes;
They murder poor parsons, and also their wives,
But soldiers at once make them run for their lives;
And wherever we march, thro' the country or town,
In ditches or cellars, the croppies lie down.

United in blood, to their country's disgrace,
They secretly shoot whom they dare not to face;
But when we can catch the sly rogues in the field,
A handful of soldiers make hundreds to yield,
And the cowards collect but to raise our renown,
For as soon as we fire the croppies lie down.

While they, in the war that unmanly they wage
On woman herself turn their blood-thirsty rage,
We'll fly to protect the dear creatures from harms,
And shelter them safely when clasp'd in our arms:
On love in a soldier no maiden will frown,
But bless the dear boys that made croppies lie down.

Should France e'er attempt, or by fraud or by guile,
Her forces to land on our emerald isle,
We'll shew that they ne'er can make free soldiers slaves,
And only possess our green fields for their graves;
Our country's applauses our triumph will crown,
While low with the French, brother, croppies lie down.

When wars and when dangers again shall be o'er,
And peace with her blessings revisit our shore;
When arms we relinquish, no longer to roam,
With pride will our families welcome us home,
And drink, as in bumpers past troubles we drown,
A health to the lads that made croppies lie down.

Anonymous

Cockles and Mussels

In Dublin's fair city,

Where the girls are so pretty,
I first set my eyes on sweet Mollie Malone.
She wheeled her wheel-barrow
Through streets broad and narrow,
Crying, 'Cockles and mussels, alive, alive, oh!

'Alive alive, oh!
Alive, alive, oh!'
Crying 'Cockles and mussels, alive, alive, oh!'

She was a fishmonger,
But sure 'twas no wonder,
For so were her father and mother before.
And they both wheeled their barrow
Through streets broad and narrow,
Crying 'Cockles and mussels, alive, alive, oh!

'Alive, alive, oh! etc.

She died of a fever,
And none could relieve her,
And that was the end of sweet Mollie Malone.
But her ghost wheels her barrow
Through streets broad and narrow,
Crying 'Cockles and mussels, alive, alive, oh!'

'Alive, alive, oh! etc.

Anonymous

The Sash my Father Wore

Sure I'm an Ulster Orangeman, from Erin's Isle I came
To see my Glasgow brethren all of honour and of fame,
And to tell them of my forefathers who fought in days of
            yore,
All on the twelfth day of July in the sash my father wore.

Chorus

It's ould, but it's beautiful, and its colours they are fine,
It was worn at Derry, Aughrim, Enniskillen and the Boyne;
My father wore it in his youth in the bygone days of yore,
And on the Twelfth I love to wear the sash my father wore.

So here I am in Glasgow town youse boys and girls to see,
And I hope that in good Orange style you all will welcome
      me,
A true blue blade that's just arrived from that dear Ulster
      shore,
All on the Twelfth day of July in the sash my father wore.

Chorus

And when I'm going to leave yeeze all 'Good luck!' to youse
      I'll say,
And as I cross the raging sea my Orange flute I'll play;
Returning to my native town, to ould Belfast once more,
To be welcomed back by Orangemen in the sash my father
      wore.

Chorus

Anonymous

I Know Where I'm Going

I know where I'm going,
I know who's going with me,
I know who I love,
But the dear knows who I'll marry.

I'll have stockings of silk,
Shoes of fine green leather,
Combs to buckle my hair
And a ring for every finger.

Feather beds are soft,
Painted rooms are bonny;

But I'd leave them all
To go with my love Johnny.

Some say he's dark,
I say he's bonny,
He's the flower of them all
My handsome, coaxing Johnny.

I know where I'm going,
I know who's going with me,
I know who I love,
But the dear knows who I'll marry.

Anonymous

Return and No Blame

Father of mine,
your sunny smile
is a dandelion
as I come once again through the door.

Our fumbled embrace
drives the wind off my shoulder
and your eyes hold a question
you will not put
as I break bread at your table
after the long seasons away from it.

Father, my head is bursting
with the things I've seen
in this strange, big world

but I don't have the words to tell you
nor the boldness to disrupt your gentle daily ways,
so I am quiet while the rashers cook,
nod and grin at any old thing.

'Oh, the boat was grand,

they took me in at Larne.'
'And a pity they didn't keep you.
Must have been a gypsy slipped you in
and I in a dead sleep one night.'

Didn't I rob you of your eyes, father,
and her of her smile? No dark blood
but the simple need to lose an uneasy love
drove me down unknown roads
where they spoke in different tongues,
drove me about the planet
till I had of it
and it of me
what we needed of each other.

Yes, father, I will have more tea
and sit here quiet in this room of my childhood
and watch while the flames flicker
the story of our distance on the wall.

Paula Meehan

The Maid of the Sweet Brown Knowe

Come all ye lads and lassies and listen to me a while,
And I'll sing for you a verse or two will cause you all to
     smile;
It's all about a young man, and I'm going to tell you now,
How he lately came a-courting of the Maid of the Sweet
     Brown Knowe.

Said he, 'My pretty fair maid, will you come along with me,
We'll both go off together, and married we will be;
We'll join our hands in wedlock bands, I'm speaking to you
     now,
And I'll do my best endeavour for the Maid of the Sweet
     Brown Knowe.'

This fair and fickle young thing, she knew not what to say,
Her eyes did shine like silver bright, and merrily did play;
She said, 'Young man, your love subdue, for I am not ready
    now,
And I'll spend another season at the foot of the Sweet Brown
    Knowe.'

Said he, 'My pretty fair maid, how can you say so,
Look down in yonder valley where my crops do gently
    grow,
Look down in yonder valley where my horses and my
    plough
Are at their daily labour at the foot of the Sweet Brown
    Knowe.'

'If they're at their daily labour, kind sir, it's not for me,
For I've heard of your behaviour, I have indeed,' said she;
'There is an Inn where you call in, I have heard the people
    say,
Where you rap and call and pay for all, and go home at the
    break of day.'

'If I rap and call and pay for all, the money is all my own,
And I'll never spend your fortune, for I hear you have got
    none.
You thought you had my poor heart broke in talking with
    me now,
But I'll leave you where I found you, at the foot of the Sweet
    Brown Knowe.'

                                                    Anonymous

Molly Bawn and Brian Oge

Come and listen to my story, Molly Bawn;
I'm bound for death or glory Molly Bawn,
For I've listed in the army
Where no more your eyes will harm me;

Faith, they kill me whilst they charm me, Molly Bawn.

Musha, Brian you're drinking now you rogue;
I know it by your blinking, Brian Oge;
But would you be the villain
For to take the Saxon shilling
And do their dirty killing, Brian Oge?
And what would all the boys say, Brian Oge?
If you turned a redcoat haythen, Brian Oge?
Go list then if it please ye,
You villain do not tease me,
Sure you'd drive a colleen crazy, Brian Oge.

It was you that drove me to it, Molly Bawn,
When you read my death you'll rue it, Molly Bawn;
When I die mid foemen wrestling,
Where the balls like hail are whistling
And bloody bayonets bristling, Molly Bawn;
And the last words I'll be speaking, Molly Bawn,
When my soul its leave is taking, Molly Bawn,
Are *gra ma chree asthoreen*,
Your sweetheart Brian Oigeen
And for you my blood is pouring, Molly Bawn.

Oh, sure I did it just to prove you, Brian Oge;
I hate you! No, I love you, Brian Oge.
But keep your heart, *a chara*,
For I'll buy you out tomorrow
Or I'll die of shame and sorrow, Brian Oge.
And to think that you should doubt me, Brian Oge,
And myself so wild about you, Brian Oge;
Would you let that thief, Phil Dorman
Come and wed me in the morning?
Faith, you might have given me warning, Brian Oge.

I am strong and hale and hearty, Molly Bawn;
I war like Bonaparty, Molly Bawn.
Sure the devil a list I listed,
The sergeant tried and missed it –

You are mine, I have confessed it, Molly Bawn.
So I'll buy for you a bonnet, Molly Bawn,
There'll be lots of ribbons on it, Molly Bawn,
And it's you that will be shining,
With your golden hair entwining;
We'll get wed and cease repining, Molly Bawn.

Oh, I'm sick and tired of scheming, Brian Oge,
'Tis yourself that thinks it's shaming, Brian Oge;
But as you did not take that shilling,
Just to save your life I'm willing –
We'll get wed – behave you villain – Brian Oge.

Anonymous

The Description of an Irish Feast
(Translated almost literally out of the original Irish)

O'Rourke's noble fare,
Will ne'er be forgot,
By those who were there,
Or those who were not.

His revels to keep,
We sup and we dine,
On seven score sheep,
Fat bullocks, and swine.

Usquebaugh to our feast
In pails was brought up,
A hundred at least,
And a madder our cup.

O there is the sport!
We rise with the light
In disorderly sort,
From snoring all night.

O how was I trick'd!
My pipe it was broke,
My pocket was pick'd
I lost my new cloak.

I'm rifled, quoth Nell,
Of mantle and kercher,
Why then fare them well,
The de'el take the searcher.

Come, harper, strike up;
But, first, by your favour,
Boy give us a cup:
Ah! this hath some savour.

O'Rourke's jolly boys
Ne'er dreamt of the matter,
Till, roused by the noise,
And musical clatter,

They bounce from their nest,
No longer will tarry,
They rise ready drest,
Without one Ave-Mary.

They dance in a round,
Cutting capers and ramping;
A mercy the ground
Did not burst with their stamping.

The floor is all wet
With leaps and with jumps,
While the water and sweat
Splish-splash in their pumps.

Bless you late and early,
Laughlin O'Enagin!
But, my hand, you dance rarely,
Margery Grinagin.

Bring straw for our bed,
Shake it down to the feet,
Then over us spread
The winnowing sheet.

To show I don't flinch,
Fill the bowl up again:
Then give us a pinch
Of your sneezing, a Yean.

Good Lord! what a sight,
After all their good cheer,
For people to fight
In the midst of their beer!

They rise from their feast,
And hot are their brains,
A cubit at least
The length of their skeans.

What stabs and what cuts,
What clattering of sticks;
What strokes on the guts,
What bastings and kicks!

With cudgels of oak,
Well harden'd in flame,
A hundred heads broke,
A hundred struck lame.

You churl, I'll maintain
My father built Lusk,
The castle of Slane,
And Carrick Drumrusk:

The Earl of Kildare,
And Moynalta his brother,
As great as they are,
I was nurst by their mother.

Ask that of old madam:
She'll tell you who's who,
As far up as Adam,
She knows it is true.

Come down with that beam,
If cudgels are scarce,
A blow on the weam,
Or a kick on the arse.

On a Curate's Complaint of Hard Duty

I march'd three miles through scorching sand,
With zeal in heart, and notes in hand;
I rode four more to Great St Mary,
Using four legs, when two were weary:
To three fair virgins I did tie men,
In the close bands of pleasing Hymen;
I dipp'd two babes in holy water,
And purified their mother after.
Within an hour and eke a half,
I preach'd three congregations deaf;
Where, thundering out, with lungs long-winded,
I chopp'd so fast, that few there minded.
My emblem, the laborious sun,
Saw all these mighty labours done
Before one race of his was run.
All this perform'd by Robert Hewit:
What mortal else could e'er go through it!

Jonathan Swift

Swift's Epitaph

Swift has sailed into his rest;

94

Savage indignation there
Cannot lacerate his breast.
Imitate him if you dare,
World-besotted traveller; he
Served human liberty.

W B Yeats

Boolavogue

At Boolavogue, as the sun was setting,
O'er the bright May meadows of Shelmalier,
A rebel hand set the heather blazing
And brought the neighbours from far and near,
Then Father Murphy, from old Kilcormack,
Spurred up the rock with a warning cry;
'Arm! Arm!' he cried, 'for I've come to lead you
For Ireland's freedom we fight or die.'

He led us on 'gainst the coming soldiers,
And the cowardly yeomen we put to flight;
'Twas at the Harrow the boys of Wexford
Showed Bookey's regiment how men could fight.
Look out for hirelings, King George of England,
Search every kingdom where breathes a slave,
For Father Murphy of County Wexford
Sweeps o'er the land like a mighty wave.

We took Camolin and Enniscorthy,
And Wexford storming drove out our foes;
'Twas at Slieve Coillte our pikes were reeking
With the crimson stream of the beaten Yeos.
At Tubberneering and Ballyellis
Full many a Hessian lay in his gore;
Ah, Father Murphy, had aid come over
The green flag floated from shore to shore.

At Vinegar Hill, o'er the pleasant Slaney,

Our heroes vainly stood back to back;
And the Yeos at Tullow took Father Murphy
And burned his body upon the rack.
God grant your glory, brave father Murphy,
And open Heaven to all your men;
The cause that called you may call tomorrow
In another fight for the Green again.

Patrick Joseph McCall

An Elegy on the Death of a Mad Dog

Good people all, of every sort,
Give ear unto my song;
And if you find it wondrous short,
It cannot hold you long.

In Islington there was a man,
Of whom the world might say,
That still a godly race he ran,
Whene'er he went to pray.

A kind and gentle heart he had,
To comfort friends and foes;
The naked every day he clad
When he put on his clothes.

And in that town a dog was found,
As many dogs there be,
Both mongrel, puppy, whelp and hound,
And curs of low degree.

This dog and man at first were friends;
But when a pique began,
The dog, to gain his private ends,
Went mad, and bit the man.

Around from all the neighbouring streets

The wondering neighbours ran,
And swore the dog had lost his wits,
To bite so good a man.

The wound it seem'd both sore and sad
To every Christian eye;
And while they swore the dog was mad,
They swore the man would die.

But soon a wonder came to light,
That show'd the rogues they lied;
The man recover'd of the bite,
The dog it was that died.

Oliver Goldsmith

from The Deserted Village

Sweet Auburn! loveliest village of the plain;
Where health and plenty cheered the labouring swain,
Where smiling spring its earliest visit paid,
And parting summer's lingering blooms delayed:
Dear lovely bowers of innocence and ease,
Seats of my youth, when every sport could please,
How often have I loitered o'er thy green,
Where humble happiness endeared each scene!
How often have I paused on every charm,
The sheltered cot, the cultivated farm,
The never-failing brook, the busy mill,
The decent church that topped the neighbouring hill,
The hawthorn bush, with seats beneath the shade,
For talking age and whispering lovers made!
How often have I blest the coming day,
When toil remitting lent its turn to play,
And all the village train, from labour free,
Led up their sports beneath the spreading tree,
While many a pastime circled in the shade,
The young contending as the old surveyed;

And many a gambol frolicked o'er the ground,
And sleights of art and feats of strength went round.
And still, as each repeated pleasure tired,
Succeeding sports the mirthful band inspired;
The dancing pair that simply sought renown,
By holding out to tire each other down;
The swain mistrustless of his smutted face,
While secret laughter tittered round the place;
The bashful virgin's side-long looks of love,
The matron's glance that would those looks reprove:
These were thy charms, sweet village! sports like these,
With sweet succession, taught even toil to please:
These round thy bowers their cheerful influence shed:
These were thy charms – but all these charms are fled.

    Sweet smiling village, loveliest of the lawn,
Thy sports are fled, and all thy charms withdrawn:
Amidst thy bowers the tyrant's hand is seen,
And desolation saddens all thy green:
One only master grasps the whole domain,
And half a tillage stints thy smiling plain.
No more thy glassy brook reflects the day,
But, choked with sedges, works its weedy way;
Along thy glades, a solitary guest,
The hollow sounding bittern guards its nest;
Amidst thy desert walks the lapwing flies,
And tires their echoes with unvaried cries;
Sunk are thy bowers in shapeless ruin all,
And the long grass o'ertops the mouldering wall;
And trembling, shrinking from the spoiler's hand,
Far, far away thy children leave the land.

    Ill fares the land, to hastening ills a prey,
Where wealth accumulates, and men decay:
Princes and lords may flourish, or may fade;
A breath can make them, as a breath has made;
But a bold peasantry, their country's pride,
When once destroyed, can never be supplied.

    A time there was, ere England's griefs began,

When every rood of ground maintained its man;
For him light labour spread her wholesome store,
Just gave what life required, but gave no more:
His best companions, innocence and health;
And his best riches, ignorance of wealth.

But times are altered; trade's unfeeling train
Usurp the land and dispossess the swain;
Along the lawn, where scattered hamlets rose,
Unwieldy wealth and cumbrous pomp repose,
And every want to opulence allied,
And every pang that folly pays to pride.
Those gentle hours that plenty bade to bloom,
Those calm desires that asked but little room,
Those healthful sports that graced the peaceful scene,
Lived in each look, and brightened all the green;
These, far departing, seek a kinder shore,
And rural mirth and manners are no more.

Sweet Auburn! parent of the blissful hour,
Thy blades forlorn confess the tyrant's power.
Here, as I take my solitary rounds
Amidst thy tangling walks and ruined grounds,
And, many a year elapsed, return to view,
Where once the cottage stood, the hawthorns grew,
Remembrance wakes with all her busy train,
Swells at my breast, and turns the past to pain.

In all my wanderings round this world of care,
In all my griefs – and God has given my share –
I still had hopes, my latest hours to crown,
Amidst these humble bowers to lay me down;
To husband out life's taper at the close,
And keep the flame from wasting by repose:
I still had hopes, for pride attends us still,
Amidst the swains to show my book-learned skill,
Around my fire an evening group to draw,
And tell of all I felt, and all I saw;
And, as an hare whom hounds and horns pursue,

Pants to the place from whence at first she flew,
I still had hopes, my long vexations past,
Here to return – and die at home at last.
O' blest retirement, friend to life's decline,
Retreats from care, that never must be mine,
How happy he who crowns in shades like these,
A youth of labour with an age of ease;
Who quits a world where strong temptations try,
And, since 'tis hard to combat, learns to fly!
For him no wretches, born to work and weep,
Explore the mine, or tempt the dangerous deep;
No surly porter stands in guilty state,
To spurn the imploring famine from the gate;
But on he moves to meet his latter end,
Angels around befriending Virtue's friend;
Bends to the grave with unperceived decay,
While resignation gently slopes the way;
And, all his prospects brightening to the last,
His heaven commences ere the world be past!

Sweet was the sound, when oft at evening's close
Up yonder hill the village murmur rose.
There, as I passed with careless steps and slow,
The mingling notes came softened from below;
The swain responsive as the milk-maid sung,
The sober herd that lowed to meet their young,
The noisy geese that gabbled o'er the pool,
The playful children just let loose from school,
The watch-dog's voice that bayed the whispering wind,
And the loud laugh that spoke the vacant mind –
These all in sweet confusion sought the shade,
And filled each pause the nightingale had made.
But now the sounds of population fail,
No cheerful murmurs fluctuate in the gale,
No busy steps the grass-grown foot-way tread,
For all the bloomy flush of life is fled.
All but yon widowed, solitary thing,
That feebly bends beside the plashy spring:
She, wretched matron, forced in age, for bread,

To strip the brook with mantling cresses spread,
To pick her wintry faggot from the thorn,
To seek her nightly shed, and weep 'til morn;
She only left of all the harmless train,
The sad historian of the pensive plain.

Near yonder copse, where once the garden smiled,
And still where many a garden flower grows wild;
There, where a few torn shrubs the place disclose,
The village preacher's modest mansion rose.
A man he was to all the country dear,
And passing rich with forty pounds a year;
Remote from towns he ran his godly race,
Nor e'er had changed, nor wished to change his place;
Unpracticed he to fawn, or seek for power,
By doctrines fashioned to the varying hour;
Far other aims his heart had learned to prize,
More skilled to raise the wretched than to rise.
His house was known to all the vagrant train;
He chid their wanderings but relieved their pain:
The long-remembered beggar was his guest,
Whose beard descending swept his aged breast;
The ruined spendthrift, now no longer proud,
Claimed kindred there, and had his claims allowed;
The broken soldier, kindly bade to stay,
Sat by the fire, and talked the night away,
Wept o'er his wounds or, tales of sorrow done,
Shouldered his crutch and showed how fields were won.
Pleased with his guests, the good man learned to glow,
And quite forgot their vices in their woe;
Careless their merits or their faults to scan
His pity gave ere charity began.

Thus to relieve the wretched was his pride,
And e'en his failings leaned to Virtue's side;
But in his duty prompt at every call,
He watched and wept, he prayed and felt for all;
And, as a bird each fond endearment tries
To tempt its new-fledged offspring to the skies,

He tried each art, reproved each dull delay,
Allured to brighter worlds, and led the way.

Beside the bed where parting life was laid,
And sorrow, guilt, and pain by turns dismayed,
The reverend champion stood. At his control
Despair and anguish fled the struggling soul;
Comfort came down the trembling wretch to raise,
And his last faltering accents whispered praise.

At church, with meek and unaffected grace,
His looks adorned the venerable place;
Truth from his lips prevailed with double sway,
And fools, who came to scoff, remained to pray.
The service past, around the pious man,
With steady zeal, each honest rustic ran;
Even children followed with endearing wile,
And plucked his gown to share the good man's smile.
His steady smile a parent's warmth exprest;
Their welfare pleased him, and their cares distrest:
To them his heart, his love, his griefs were given,
But all his serious thoughts had rest in heaven.
As some tall cliff that lifts its awful form,
Swells from the vale, and midway leaves the storm,
Though round its breast the rolling clouds are spread,
Eternal sunshine settles on its head.

Beside yon straggling fence that skirts the way,
With blossomed furze unprofitably gay,
There, in his noisy mansion, skilled to rule,
The village master taught his little school.
A man severe he was, and stern to view;
I knew him well, and every truant knew;
Well had the boding tremblers learned to trace
The day's disasters in his morning face;
Full well they laughed with counterfeited glee
At all his jokes, for many a joke had he;
Full well the busy whisper circling round
Conveyed the dismal tidings when he frowned.

Yet he was kind, or, if severe in aught,
The love he bore to learning was in fault;
The village all declared how much he knew:
'Twas certain he could write, and cipher too;
Lands he could measure, terms and tides presage,
And even the story ran that he could gauge;
In arguing, too, the parson owned his skill,
For, even though vanquished, he could argue still;
While words of learned length and thundering sound
Amazed the gazing rustics ranged around;
And still they gazed, and still the wonder grew,
That one small head could carry all he knew.

   But past is all his fame. The very spot
Where many a time he triumphed, is forgot.

Oliver Goldsmith

The Street

I love the flags that pave the walk.
I love the mud between,
The funny figures drawn in chalk.
I love to hear the sound
Of drays upon their round,
Of horses and their clock-like-walk
I love to watch the corner-people gawk
And hear what underlies their idle talk.

I love to hear the music of the rain.
I love to hear the sound
Of yellow waters flushing in the main.
I love the breaks between
When little boys begin
To sail their paper galleons in the drain.
Grey clouds sail west and silver tips remain.
The street, thank God, is bright and clean again.

Here, within a single little street,

Is everything that is
Of pomp and blessed poverty made sweet
And all that is of love
Of man and God above,
Of happiness and sorrow and conceit,
Of tragedy and death and bitter-sweet,
Of hope, despair, illusion and defeat.

A golden mellow peace forever clings
Along the little street.
There are so very many lasting things
Beyond the wall of strife
In our beleaguered life.
There are so many lovely songs to sing
Of God and His eternal love that rings
Of simple people and of simple things.

John B. Keane

The Minstrel Boy

The minstrel boy to the war is gone,
In the ranks of death you'll find him,
His father's sword he has girded on,
And his wild harp slung behind him.
'Land of song!' said the warrior bard,
'Though all the world betrays thee,
One sword, at least, thy rights will guard,
One faithful harp shall praise thee!'

The minstrel fell! – but the foeman's chain
Could not bring his proud soul under;
The harp he loved ne'er spoke again,
For he tore its chords asunder;
And said, 'No chains shall sully thee,
Thou soul of love and bravery!
Thy songs were made for the pure and free,
They shall never sound in slavery!'

Thomas Moore

Believe Me, if all Those Endearing Young Charms

Believe me, if all those endearing young charms,
Which I gaze on so fondly today,
Were to change by tomorrow, and fleet in my arms,
Like fairy gifts fading away!
Thou wouldst still be adored, as this moment thou art,
Let thy loveliness fade as it will,
And around the dear ruin each wish of my heart
Would entwine itself verdantly still.

It is not while beauty and youth are thine own,
And thy cheeks unprofaned by a tear,
That the fervour and faith of a soul may be known,
To which time will but make thee more dear!
Oh the heart that has truly loved never forgets,
But as truly loves on to the close,
As the sunflower turns to her god when he sets
The same look which she turned when he rose!

Thomas Moore

The Last Rose of Summer

'Tis the last rose of summer,
Left blooming alone;
All her lovely companions
Are faded and gone;
No flower of her kindred,
No rose bud is nigh
To reflect back her blushes,
Or give sigh for sigh!

I'll not leave thee, thou lone one!
To pine on the stem;
Since the lovely are sleeping,

Go, sleep thou with them;
Thus kindly I scatter
Thy leaves o'er the bed,
Where thy mates of the garden
Lie scentless and dead.

So soon may I follow,
When friendships decay,
And from love's shining circle
Thy gems drop away!
When true hearts lie withered,
And fond ones are flown,
Oh! who would inhabit
This bleak world alone?

Thomas Moore

The Song of Fionnuala

Silent, O Moyle! be the roar of thy water,
Break not, ye breezes, your chain of repose,
While, murmuring mournfully, Lir's lonely daughter
Tells to the night-star her tale of woes.
When shall the swan, her death-note singing,
Sleep, with wings in darkness furled?
When will heaven, its sweet bell ringing,
Call my spirit from this stormy world?

Sadly, O Moyle! to thy winter wave weeping,
Fate bids me languish long ages away!
Yet still in her darkness doth Erin lie sleeping,
Still doth the pure light its dawning delay!
When will that day-star, mildly springing,
Warm our isle with peace and love?
When will heaven, its sweet bell ringing,
Call my spirit to the fields above?

Thomas Moore

Between

As we fall into step I ask a penny for your thoughts.
'Oh, nothing,' you say, 'well, nothing so easily bought.'

Sliding into the rhythm of your silence, I almost forget
how lonely I'd been until that autumn morning we met.

At bedtime up along my childhood's stairway, tongues
of fire cast shadows. Too earnest, too highstrung.

My desire is endless: others ended when I'd only started.
Then, there was you: so whole-hog, so wholehearted.

Think of the thousands of nights and the shadows
    fought.
And the mornings of light. I try to read your thought.

In the strange openness of your face, I'm powerless.
Always this love. Always this infinity between us.

Micheal O'Siadhail

The Old Story Over Again

When I was a maid,
Nor of lovers afraid,
My mother cried, 'Girl, never listen to men.'
Her lectures were long,
But I thought her quite wrong,
And I said, 'Mother, whom should I listen to, then?'

Now teaching, in turn,
What I could never learn,
I find, like my mother, my lessons all vain;
Men ever deceive –
Silly maidens believe,
And still 'tis the old story over again.

So humbly they woo,
What can poor maidens do
But keep them alive when they swear they must die?
Ah! who can forbear,
As they weep in despair,
The crocodile tears in compassion to dry?

Yet, wedded at last,
When the honeymoon's past,
The lovers forsake us, the husbands remain;
Our vanity's checked,
And we ne'er can expect
They will tell us the old story over again.

James Kenney

Woman

Not she with traitorous kiss her Saviour stung,
Not she denied Him with unholy tongue;
She, while apostles shrank, could dangers brave,
Last at the cross and earliest at the grave.

Eaton Stannard Barrett

John Kinsella's Lament for Mrs Mary Moore

A bloody and a sudden end,
Gunshot or a noose,
For Death who takes what man would keep,
Leaves what man would lose.
He might have had my sister,
My cousins by the score,
But nothing satisfied the fool
But my dear Mary Moore,
None other knows what pleasures man
At table or in bed.

What shall I do for pretty girls
Now my old bawd is dead?

Though stiff to strike a bargain,
Like an old Jew man,
Her bargain struck we laughed and talked
And emptied many a can;
And O! but she had stories,
Though not for the priest's ear,
To keep the soul of man alive,
Banish age and care,
And being old she put a skin
On everything she said.
What shall I do for pretty girls
Now my old bawd is dead?

The priests have got a book that says
But for Adam's sin
Eden's Garden would be there
And I there within.
No expectation fails there,
No pleasing habit ends,
No man grows old, no girl grows cold,
But friends walk by friends.
Who quarrels over halfpennies
That plucks the trees for bread?
What shall I do for pretty girls
Now my old bawd is dead?

W B Yeats

The Belfast Cockabendy

You lads and lasses brisk and gay
I pray you pay attention
And listen now to what I'll say
Perhaps some things I'll mention
Which may your jealousy provoke

Or else 'twill please your fancy
We will pass it over as a joke
And I will kiss my Nancy.

When you come to Belfast town
Come not without some shillings
And you had better bring a pound
To make the lasses willing
Then if you wish a bit of fish
Go take a drop of brandy
And if you choose they'll not refuse
To play up cockabendy.

As I was walking up North Street
I being in good apparel
I on the way did chance to meet
A smiling pretty girl
Straight to a dram shop then we went
To take a drop of brandy
And home we went with one consent
To play with cockabendy.

Then with my smiling little friend
We being but one couple
A crown or two I had to spend
Because I spoiled her ruffle
My watch my chain and golden seal
While I was full of brandy
Out of my fob they were conveyed
While playing cockabendy.

Then up to Carrick Hill I strayed
In serious contemplation
Bestowing on the smiling maid
Many an execration
A light I spied and in I hied
Where they were drinking brandy
And a bonny lass reached me a glass
And welcomed cockabendy.

I then lay down to take a sleep
And swore away all sorrow
Determining from home to keep
Until the other morrow
When I awoke my hat and coat
I found were pledged for brandy
And I got fire without a smoke
While playing cockabendy.

The two last crowns which I had found
Went to release my garments
They searched my fob for other Joes
Which caused me much alarm
The wicked Queen did curse and swear
That she should have more brandy
And I paid the piper let who will dance
To the tune of cockabendy.

When over the long bridge I strayed
As I thought free from danger
I turned in to see a maid
To whom I was no stranger
Said if you run your pretty face
Trust for one pint of brandy
I'll surely pay next market day
And we'll play cockabendy.

It's I presume you're short of cash
The damsel she retorted
And you have lost your silver watch
Wherever you resorted
Begone you dirty drunken sot
Where e'er you drank your brandy
Then right across the nose she struck
Poor simple cockabendy.

The Belfast lads they say are prone
For to love the lasses
The lasses I am sure are prone

For to love their glasses
Botany Bay's the place they take their tea
Carrick Hill their brandy
And Mill Street is a bonny place
For playing cockabendy.

Anonymous

Autumn Journal
Section XVI

Why do we like being Irish? Partly because
It gives us a hold on the sentimental English
As members of a world that never was,
Baptised with fairy water;
And partly because Ireland is small enough
To be still thought of with a family feeling,
And because the waves are rough
That split her from a more commercial culture;
And because one feels that here at least one can
Do local work which is not at the world's mercy
And that on this tiny stage with luck a man
Might see the end of one particular action.
It is self-deception of course;
There is no immunity in this island either;
A cart that is drawn by somebody else's horse
And carrying goods to somebody else's market.
The bombs in the turnip sack, the sniper from the roof,
Griffith, Connolly, Collins, where have they brought us?
Ourselves alone! Let the round tower stand aloof
In a world of bursting mortar!
Let the school-children fumble their sums
In a half-dead language;
Let the censor be busy on the books; pull down the
    Georgian slums;
Let the games be played in Gaelic.
Let them grow beet-sugar; let them build
A factory in every hamlet;

Let them pigeon-hole the souls of the killed
Into sheep and goats, patriots and traitors.
And the North, where I was a boy,
Is still the North, veneered with the grime of Glasgow,
Thousands of men whom nobody will employ
Standing at the corners, coughing.
And the street-children play on the wet
Pavement – hopscotch or marbles;
And each rich family boasts a sagging tennis-net
On a spongy lawn beside a dripping shrubbery.
The smoking chimneys hint
At prosperity round the corner
But they make their Ulster linen from foreign lint
And the money that comes in goes out to make more
    money.
A city built upon mud;
A culture built upon profit;
Free speech nipped in the bud,
The minority always guilty.
Why should I want to go back
To you, Ireland, my Ireland?
The blots on the page are so black
That they cannot be covered with shamrock.
I hate your grandiose airs,
Your sob-stuff, your laugh and your swagger,
Your assumption that everyone cares
Who is the king of your castle.
Castles are out of date,
The tide flows round the children's sandy fancy;
Put up what flag you like, it is too late
To save your soul with bunting.
Odi atque amo:
Shall we cut this name on trees with a rusty dagger?
Her mountains are still blue, her rivers flow
Bubbling over the boulders.
She is both a bore and a bitch;
Better close the horizon,
Send her no more fantasy, no more longings which
Are under a fatal tariff.

For common sense is the vogue
And she gives her children neither sense nor money
Who slouch around the world with a gesture and a
    brogue
And a faggot of useless memories.

Louis MacNiece

Love Song

Sweet in her green dell the Flower of Beauty slumbers
Lulled by the faint breezes sighing through her hair;
Sleeps she and hears not the melancholy numbers
Breathed to my sad lute 'mid the lonely air.

Down from the high cliffs the rivulet is teeming
To wind round the willow banks that lure him from above;
O that in tears, from my rocky prison streaming,
I too could glide to the bower of my love!

Ah where the woodbines with sleepy arms have wound her,
Opes she her eyelids at the dream of my lay,
Listening, like the dove, while the fountains echo round her,
To her lost mate's call in the forests far away.

Come, then, my bird! For the peace thou ever bearest,
Still heaven's messenger of comfort to me,
Come, this fond bosom, O faithfulest and fairest,
Bleeds with its death-wound its wound of love for thee.

George Darley

The Burial of Sir John Moore

Not a drum was heard, not a funeral note,
    As his corse to the rampart we hurried;
Not a soldier discharged his farewell shot
    O'er the grave where our hero we buried.

We buried him darkly at dead of night,
The sods with our bayonets turning,
By the struggling moonbeam's misty light,
And the lantern dimly burning.

No useless coffin enclosed his breast,
Not in sheet or in shroud we wound him;
But he lay like a warrior taking his rest,
With his martial cloak around him.

Few and short were the prayers we said,
And we spoke not a word of sorrow;
But we steadfastly gazed on the face that was dead,
And we bitterly thought of the morrow.

We thought, as we hollowed his narrow bed,
And smoothed down his lonely pillow,
That the foe and stranger would tread o'er his head,
And we far away on the billow!

Lightly they'll talk of the spirit that's gone,
And o'er his cold ashes upbraid him –
But little he'll reck, if they let him sleep on
In the grave where a Briton has laid him.

But half of our heavy task was done,
When the clock struck the hour for retiring;
And we heard the distant and random gun
That the foe was sullenly firing.

Slowly and sadly we laid him down,
From the field of his fame, fresh or gory;
We carved not a line, we raised not a stone –
But we left him alone in his glory!

Charles Wolfe

Come Back, Paddy Reilly

The Garden of Eden has vanished they say,
But I know the lie of it still.

Just turn to the left at the bridge of Finea,
And stop when half-way to Cootehill.
'Tis there I will find it, I know sure enough,
When fortune had come to my call.
Oh, the grass it is green around Ballyjamesduff,
And the blue sky is over it all!
And tones that are tender and tones that are gruff
Are whispering over the sea,
'Come back, Paddy Reilly, to Balljamesduff,
Come home, Paddy Reilly, to me.'

My mother once told me that when I was born,
The day that I first saw the light,
I looked down the street on that very first morn
And gave a great crow of delight.
Now most new-born babies appear in a huff
And start with a sorrowful squall,
But I knew I was born in Ballyjamesduff
And that's why I smiled on them all!
The baby's a man now, he's toil-worn and tough,
Still, whispers come over the sea,
'Come back, Paddy Reilly, to Ballyjamesduff,
Come home, Paddy Reilly, to me.'

The night that we danced by the light o' the moon,
Wid Phil to the fore wid his flute,
When Phil threw his lip over 'Come agin soon',
He'd dance the foot out o' yer boot!
The day that I took long Magee by the scruff,
For slanderin' Rosie Kilrain;
Then marchin' him straight out of Ballyjamesduff,
Assisted him into a drain.
Oh! sweet are me dreams as the dudeen I puff,
Of whisperings over the sea:
'Come back, Paddy Reilly, to Ballyjamesduff,
Come home, Paddy Reilly, to me.'

I've loved the young weeman of every land,
That always came easy to me;

Just barrin' the belles of the Blackamore brand,
And the chocolate shapes of Feegee.
But that sort of love is a moonshining stuff,
And never will addle me brain;
For bells will be ringin' in Ballyjamesduff
For me and me Rosie Kilrain.
And all through their glamour, their gas, and their guff,
A whisper comes over the sea:
'Come back, Paddy Reilly, to Ballyjamesduff,
Come home, Paddy Reilly, to me.'

Percy French

What will you do, Love?

'What will you do, love, when I am going,
With white sail flowing,
The seas beyond? –
What will you do, love, when waves divide us,
And friends may chide us
For being fond?'
'Though waves divide us, and friends be chiding,
In faith abiding,
I'll still be true!
And I'll pray for thee on the stormy ocean,
In deep devotion –
That's what I'll do!'

'What would you do, love, if distant tidings
Thy fond confidings
Should undermine? –
And I, abiding 'neath sultry skies,
Should think other eyes
Were as bright as thine?'
'Oh, name it not! – though guilt and shame
Were on thy name,
I'd still be true:
But that heart of thine – should another share it –

117

I could not bear it!
What would I do?'

'What would you do, love, when home returning,
With hopes high-burning,
With wealth for you,
If my bark, which bounded o'er foreign foam,
Should be lost near home –
Ah! what would you do?'
'So thou wert spared – I'd bless the morrow
In want and sorrow,
That left me you;
And I'd welcome thee from the wasting billow,
This heart thy pillow –
That's what I'd do!'

Samuel Lover

The Low-Backed Car

When first I saw sweet Peggy,
'Twas on a market day,
A low-backed car she drove, and sat
Upon a truss of hay;
But when that hay was blooming grass,
And decked with flowers of Spring,
No flow'r was there that could compare
With the blooming girl I sing.
As she sat in the low-backed car –
The man at the turnpike bar
Never asked for the toll,
But just rubbed his ould poll
And looked after the low-backed car.

In battle's wild commotion,
The proud and mighty Mars,
With hostile scythes, demands his tithes
Of death – in warlike cars;
While Peggy, peaceful goddess,

Has darts in her bright eye,
That knock men down, in the market town,
As right and left they fly –
While she sits in her low-backed car,
Than battle more dangerous far –
For the doctor's art
Cannot cure the heart
That is hit from that low-backed car.

Sweet Peggy, round her car, sir,
Has strings of ducks and geese,
But the scores of hearts she slaughters
By far outnumber these;
While she among her poultry sits,
Just like a turtle-dove,
Well worth the cage, I do engage,
Of the blooming God of Love!
While she sits in her low-backed car
The lovers come near and far,
And envy the chicken
That Peggy is pickin',
As she sits in her low-backed car.

Oh, I'd rather own that car, sir,
With Peggy by my side,
Than a coach-and-four and gold galore,
And a lady for my bride;
For the lady would sit forninst me,
On a cushion made with taste,
While Peggy would sit beside me
With my arm around her waist –
While we drove in the low-backed car,
To be married by Father Maher,
Oh, my heart would beat high
At her glance and her sigh –
Though it beat in a low-backed car.

Samuel Lover

Hy-Brasail – The Isle of the Blest

On the ocean that hollows the rocks where ye dwell,
A shadowy land has appeared, as they tell;
Men thought it a region of sunshine and rest,
And they called it Hy-Brasail, the isle of the blest.
From year unto year on the ocean's blue rim,
The beautiful spectre showed lovely and dim;
The golden clouds curtained the deep where it lay,
And it looked like an Eden, away, far away!

A peasant who heard of the wonderful tale,
In the breeze of the Orient loosened his sail;
From Ara, the holy, he turned to the west,
For though Ara was holy, Hy-Brasail was blest.
He heard not the voices that called from the shore –
He heard not the rising wind's menacing roar;
Home, kindred, and safety he left on that day,
And he sped to Hy-Brasail, away, far away!

Morn rose on the deep, and that shadowy isle,
O'er the faint rim of distance, reflected its smile;
Noon burned on the wave, and that shadowy shore
Seemed lovelily distant, and faint as before;
Lone evening came down on the wanderer's track,
And to Ara again he looked timidly back;
Oh, far on the verge of the ocean it lay,
Yet the isle of the blest was away, far away!

Rash dreamer, return! Oh, ye winds of the main,
Bear him back to his own peaceful Ara again.
Rash fool! for a vision of fanciful bliss,
To barter thy calm life of labour and peace.
The warning of reason was spoken in vain;
He never revisited Ara again!
Night fell on the deep, amidst tempest and spray,
And he died on the waters, away, far away!

Gerald Griffin

120

Lines Addressed to a Seagull

White bird of the tempest! O beautiful thing!
With the bosom of snow and the motionless wing,
Now sweeping the billow, now floating on high,
Now bathing thy plumes in the light of the sky,
Now poising o'er ocean thy delicate form,
Now breasting the surge with thy bosom so warm,
Now darting aloft with a heavenly scorn,
Now shooting along like a ray of the morn,
Now lost in the folds of the cloud-curtained dome,
Now floating abroad like a flake of the foam,

Now silently poised o'er the war of the main,
Like the spirit of Charity brooding o'er pain,
Now gliding with pinion all silently furled,
Like an angel descending to comfort the world!
Thou seem'st to my spirit, as upward I gaze,
And see thee, now clothéd in mellowest rays,
Now lost in the storm-driven vapours that fly
Like hosts that are routed across the broad sky,
Like a pure spirit true to its virtue and faith,
Mid the tempests of Nature, of passion, and death!

Rise, beautiful emblem of purity, rise!
On the sweet winds of heaven to thine own brilliant
   skies;
Still higher – still higher– till lost to our sight,
Thou hidest thy wings in a mantle of light;
And I think, how a pure spirit gazing on thee,
Must long for the moment – the joyous and free –
When the soul disembodied from nature shall spring
Unfettered at once to her Maker and King;
When the bright day of service and suffering past,
Shapes fairer than thine shall shine round her at last,
While, the standard of battle triumphantly furled,
She smiles like a victor, serene on the world!

Gerald Griffin

The Irish Emigrant

I'm sitting on the stile, Mary,
Where we sat side by side,
On a bright May morning, long ago,
When first you were my bride.
The corn was springing fresh and green,
And the lark sang loud and high,
And the red was on your lip, Mary,
And the love-light in your eye.
The place is little changed, Mary,
The day is bright as then,
The lark's loud song is in my ear,
And the corn is green again;
But I miss the soft clasp of your hand,
And the breath warm on my cheek,
And I still keep listening for the words
You nevermore may speak,
You nevermore may speak.

'Tis but a step down yonder lane,
The little church stands near –
The church where we were wed, Mary –
I see the spire from here;
But the graveyard lies between, Mary,
My step might break your rest,
Where you, my darling, lie asleep
With your baby on your breast.

I'm very lonely now, Mary,
The poor make no new friends;
But, oh, they love the better still
The few our Father sends.
And you were all I had, Mary,
My blessing and my pride;
There's nothing left to care for now
Since my poor Mary died.

Yours was the good brave heart, Mary,
That still kept hoping on,
When trust in God had left my soul,
And half my strength was gone.
There was comfort ever on your lip,
And the kind look on your brow;
I bless you, Mary, for that same,
Though you can't hear me now.

I'm bidding you a long farewell,
My Mary, kind and true!
But I'll not forget you darling,
In the land I'm going to.
They say there's bread and work for all,
And the sun shines always there;
But I'll not forget old Ireland
Were it fifty times as fair.

Lady Dufferin

Throwing the Beads

A mother at Shannon, waving to her young
Son setting out from North Kerry, flung
A rosary beads out to the tarmac
Suddenly as a lifebelt hurled from a pier.
Don't forget to say your prayers in Manhattan.
Dangling between ticket and visa,
She saw the bright crucifix among skyscrapers,
Shielding him from harm in streets out of serials,
Comforting as a fat Irish cop in a gangster film
Rattling his baton along a railing after dark.

Sean Dunne

My Life, My Voice, My Story

The moon blackened at my birth

and long night's cry began.
Pain became my bed-fellow
and despair my song.
God disappeared behind the clouds;
I lost my star-signpost to hope.

Light found a chink to peep through
when poems were read to my starved soul.
Loneliness brought moments of repose;
lines poured through my veins
and love glimmered on my tongue.
Little birds became my inspiration.

Left with my own silent melody,
I painted notes of long-forgotten tunes
trembling in my trapped heart.
Light burst through my dark mouth
and myriad songs flew heavenwards.
I was poised for flight ...

Davoren Hanna

The Nameless One

Roll forth, my song, like the rushing river
That sweeps along to the mighty sea;
God will inspire me while I deliver
My soul to thee!

Tell thou the world, when my bones lie whitening
Amid the lost homes of youth and eld,
That there was once one whose veins ran lightning
No eye beheld.

Tell how his boyhood was one drear night-hour,
How shone for *him*, through his griefs and gloom,
No star of all heaven sends to light our
Path to the tomb.

Roll on, my song, and to after ages
Tell how, disdaining all earth can give,
He would have taught men, from wisdom's pages,
The way to live.

And tell how trampled, derided, hated,
And worn by weakness, disease and wrong,
He fled for shelter to God, who mated
His soul with song –

With song which alway, sublime or vapid,
Flowed like a rill in the morning-beam,
Perchance not deep, but intense and rapid –
A mountain stream.

Tell how this nameless, condemned for years long
To herd with demons from hell beneath,
Saw things that made him, with groans and tears, long
For even death.

Go on to tell how, with genius wasted,
Betrayed in friendship, befooled in love,
With spirit shipwrecked, and young hopes blasted,
He still, still strove.

Till, spent with toil, dreeing death for others,
And some whose hands should have wrought for *him*;
(If children live not for sires and mothers),
His mind grew dim.

And he fell far through that pit abysmal,
The gulf and grave of Maginn and Burns,
And pawned his soul for the devil's dismal
Stock of returns.

But yet redeemed it in days of darkness,
And shapes and signs of the final wrath,
When death, in hideous and ghastly starkness,
Stood on his path.

And tell how now, amid wreck and sorrow,

And want, and sickness, and houseless nights,
He bides in calmness the silent morrow,
That no ray lights.

And lives he still, then? Yes! Old and hoary
At thirty-nine, from despair and woe,
He lives, enduring what future story
Will never know.

Him grant a grave to, ye pitying noble,
Deep in your bosoms! There let him dwell!
He, too, had tears for all souls in trouble,
Here and in hell.

James Clarence Mangan

Gone in the Wind

Mangan claimed this to be a translation from the German poet Friedrich Ruckert. It is mostly Mangan – as are most of his translations.

Solomon! where is thy throne? It is gone in the wind.
Babylon! where is thy might? It is gone in the wind.
Like the swift shadows of noon, like the dreams of the Blind,
Vanish the glories and pomps of the earth in the wind.

Man! canst thou build upon aught in the pride of thy mind?
Wisdom will teach thee that nothing can tarry behind;
Though there be thousand bright actions embalmed and en-
        shrined,
Myriads and millions of brighter are snow in the wind.

Solomon! where is thy throne? It is gone in the wind.
Babylon! where is thy might? It is gone in the wind.
All that the genius of man hath achieved or designed
Waits but its hour to be dealt with as dust by the wind.

Say, what is Pleasure? A phantom, a mask undefined.
Science? An almond, whereof we can pierce but the rind.
Honor and Affluence? Firmans that fortune hath signed

Only to glitter and pass on the wings of the wind.

Solomon! where is thy throne? It is gone in the wind.
Babylon! where is thy might? It is gone in the wind.
Who is the Fortunate? He who in anguish hath pined!
He shall rejoice when his relics are dust in the wind!

Mortal! be careful with what thy best hopes are entwined;
Woe to the miners for Truth – where the Lampless have
       mined!
Woe to the seekers on earth for – what none ever find!
They and their trust shall be scattered like leaves on the
       wind.

Solomon! where is thy throne? It is gone in the wind.
Babylon! where is thy might? It is gone in the wind.
Happy in death are they only whose hearts have consigned
All Earth's affections and longings and cares to the wind.

Pity, thou, reader! the madness of poor Humankind,
Raving of Knowledge – and Satan so busy to blind!
Raving of Glory – like me – for the garlands I bind
(Garlands of song) are but gathered, and – strewn in the
       wind!

Solomon! where is thy throne? It is gone in the wind.
Babylon! where is thy might? It is gone in the wind.
I, Abul-Namez, must rest; for my fire hath declined,
And I hear voices from Hades like bells on the wind!

James Clarence Mangan

Shapes and Signs

I see black dragons mount the sky,
I see earth yawn beneath my feet –
I feel within the asp, the worm

That will not sleep and cannot die,
Fair though may show the winding-sheet!
I hear all night as through a storm
Hoarse voices calling, calling
My name upon the wind –
All omens monstrous and appalling
Affright my guilty mind.

I exult alone in one wild hour –
That hour in which the red cup drowns
The memories it anon renews
In ghastlier guise, in fiercer power –
Then fancy brings me golden crowns,
And visions of all brilliant hues
Lap my lost soul in gladness,
Until I wake again,
And the dark lava-fires of madness
Once more sweep through my brain.

James Clarence Mangan

Siberia

In Siberia's wastes
The ice-wind's breath
Woundeth like the toothed steel.
Lost Siberia doth reveal
Only blight and death –

Blight and death alone.
No Summer shines.
Night is interblent with Day.
In Siberia's wastes alway
The blood blackens, the heart pines.

In Siberia's wastes
No tears are shed,
For they freeze within the brain.

Nought is felt but dullest pain,
Pain acute, yet dead;

Pain as in a dream,
When years go by
Funeral-paced, yet fugitive,
When man lives, and doth not live,
Doth not live – nor die.

In Siberia's wastes
Are sands and rocks.
Nothing blooms of green or soft,
But the snow-peaks rise aloft
And the gaunt ice-blocks.

And the exile there
Is one with those;
They are part, and he is part,
For the sands are in his heart,
And the killing snows.

Therefore in those wastes
None curse the Czar.
Each man's tongue is cloven by
The North Blast, that heweth nigh
With sharp scimitar.

And such doom each drees,
Till, hunger-gnawn,
And cold-slain, he at length sinks there,
Yet scarce more a corpse than ere
His last breath was drawn.

James Clarence Mangan

Carrigafoyle

On the banks of the Shannon from Cavan to Clare
There are ruins and relics enough and to spare
There are castles, and abbeys, and anchorite cells,

With cromlechs and forts and miraculous wells,
And each has its story of fame and of glory,
That clings like the moss to these monuments hoary.
There are songs that are merry and songs that are sad,
There are memories of good men and stories of bad;
But the drollest I've heard for a very long while
Is the tale of O'Connor of Carrigafoyle.

Now the castle of Carrigafoyle, by the way,
Is in Kerry opposite Poulnasherry Bay,
Where reigned long ago with much glory and honour
O'Connor the king of Iraghticonnor;
And there was not a merrier mansion in Kerry,
From famed Knockanore to Portmagee Ferry,
With plenty of liquor and money to kick, or
To burn if you wanted to make it go quicker:
For whiskey was cheaper than paraffin oil
In the days of O'Connor of Carrigafoyle.

Now at one time this King when in Paris he saw
A gem in a shop without blemish or flaw,
The colour was green, and the cutting was clean,
Ah! 'Twas one of the finest he had ever seen.
He bought it and paid, but in truth I'm afraid
That he did not pay then, but a bargain he made
To pay in a year, and he swore on his honour
If he did not he'd forfeit Iraghticonnor.
Then he came back to Kerry, and, just as he thought,
His friends were amazed at the fine jewel he brought.

The McAuliffes, O'Deas and the Hickies of Clare
Were jealous, and so was O'Sullivan Beare,
The FitzGeralds of Glin, and the Stacks of Kilflyn,
They had nothing to do but bear it and grin
So he flashed it this way for a year and a day,
'Till it flashed through his mind he'd forgotten to pay,
So he gave up his lands as a gentleman ought to,
But his castle he kept for 'twas built on the water:
And there he used sit in a turret alone,
Bewailing his folly, and cursing the stone.

He was crying in rage one day when a page
Approaching said – 'Why, sire, in tears at your age?'
But he answered: 'My lad, 'tis no wonder I'm sad,
For if you did as I did you'd feel just as bad.
For this pitiful pebble I've bartered the soil
Of Iraghticonnor and Carrigafoyle.

'This trinket,' he cried, 'that you see on my ear
Was bought for a realm – don't you think it was dear?
From the Cashen to Clare did my forefathers share
But my property now is just fifty feet square.
Ah! Why do I croak?' With his sword as he spoke
He severed the lobe from his ear with a stroke;
Then jumped from his seat, took the gem and the meat
And hurled them both to the sands at his feet.
A tiny spot showed where they rested a while
Ere they sank in the quicksands of Carrigafoyle.

'By Gor, Sire,' says the page, 'I now know the way
To get back your estates, if you do as I say,'
'I certainly will,' says the king, 'if I can.'
'Ah! 'Tis easy,' the lad said, 'and this is the plan.'
So there on the spot he unfolded the plot,
And the King said he'd see could he work it or not:
So he started at once, and he headed for France,
Where he called on the jeweller, as if 'twas by chance,
And he wore his long hair hanging down, which I'm told
Was the usual custom in Ireland of old.

But he must have determined when leaving his home
To do like the Romans while they were in Rome
So to pass for a Frenchman while he was in Gaul,
He said he was going that night to a ball,
And he wanted a fine chain of gold for his hair
Like the nobles of France in those days used to wear;
When French cavaliers bound their locks it appears,
With a chain that they hung from the lobes of their ears.

He said that he wanted one surely that night;

'But be careful,' he said, 'that the size is alright.'
The jeweller told him that they needn't worry,
He'd have the chain specially made in a hurry;
But the King said that he would like some guarantee
'Twould be ready for fear he'd be late, do you see,
'To be sure,' says the jeweller, 'don't say one word more,
Can't we make the same bargain we made as before?'

He wrote out an agreement agreeing to bring
That evening a chain the right size for the King
And if 'twas not ready that evening at ten
O'Connor could have his estates back again.
At last ten o'clock came and to shorten my song
He brought him a chain about ten inches long
'I'm afraid 'tis a little too short,' says the Don.
'Nonsense man,' says the Frenchman, 'let me try it on.'

He felt the King's hair, and he searched everywhere;
And at last he exclaimed, 'But your ear isn't there.'
The king answered, 'No, for I left it below
In the quicksands of Carrig a fortnight ago
And I'll trouble you now to go lively and bring
A chain that will fit, not like this little thing
But one that will reach every inch of the way
From Carrigafoyle to the Rue de la Paix.'

To finish my story the jeweller he swore
Such a swindle he never encountered before.
He cursed and he fumed, he groaned and he whined
When the monarch produced the agreement he signed
To deliver a chain to O'Connor that night,
That would hang from his left ear and reach to his right;
But when one ear was gone and he had only one
It was damn hard to see how that thing could be done.
So they settled the case, as the legend relates,
By the King getting back all his Irish estates
And he reigned ever after the lord of the soil
Of Iraghticonnor and Carrigafoyle.

The O'Rahilly

The Mountains of Mourne

Oh, Mary, this London's a wonderful sight,
Wid people here workin' by day and by night:
They don't sow potatoes, nor barley, nor wheat,
But there's gangs o' them diggin' for gold in the street –
At least, when I axed them, that's what I was told,
So I just took a hand at this diggin' for gold,
But for all that I found there I might as well be
Where the Mountains of Mourne sweep down to the sea.

I believe that, when writin', a wish you expressed
As to how the fine ladies in London were dressed.
Well, if you'll believe me, when axed to a ball,
They don't wear a top to their dresses at all!
Oh! I've seen them meself, and you could not in thrath,
Say if they were bound for a ball or a bath –
Don't be startin' them fashions now Mary Machree,
Where the Mountains o' Mourne sweep down to the sea.

I seen England's king from the top of a 'bus –
I never knew him, though he means to know us:
And though by the Saxon we once were oppressed,
Still, I cheered – God forgive me – I cheered wid the rest.
And now that he's visited Erin's green shore,
We'll be much better friends then we've been heretofore,
When we've got all we want, we're as quiet as can be
Where the Mountains o' Mourne sweep down to the sea.

You remember young Peter O'Loughlin, of course –
Well, here he is now at the head o' the force.
I met him today, I was crossin' the Strand,
And he stopped the whole street wid wan wave of his
    hand:
And there we stood talking of days that are gone,
While the whole population of London looked on;
But for all these great powers, he's wishful like me,
To be back where dark Mourne sweeps down to the sea.

There's beautiful girls here – oh, never mind!
With beautiful shapes Nature never designed,
And lovely complexions, all roses and crame,
But O'Loughlin remarked wid regard to them same:
'That if at those roses you venture to sip,
The colour might all come away on your lip,'
So I'll wait for the wild rose that's waitin' for me –
Where the Mountains o' Mourne sweep down to the sea.

Percy French

The Bells of Shandon

With deep affection and recollection
I often think of the Shandon bells,
Whose sound so wild would, in days of childhood,
Fling round my cradle their magic spells.
On this I ponder, where'er I wander,
And thus grow fonder, sweet Cork, of thee;
With thy bells of Shandon,
That sound so grand on
The pleasant waters of the river Lee.

I have heard bells chiming full many a clime in,
Tolling sublime in cathedral shrine;
While at a glib rate brass tongues would vibrate,
But all their music spoke nought to thine;
For memory dwelling on each proud swelling
Of thy belfry knelling its bold notes free,
Made the bells of Shandon
Sound far more grand on
The pleasant waters of the river Lee.

I have heard bells tolling 'old Adrian's mole' in,
Their thunder rolling from the Vatican,
With cymbals glorious, swinging uproarious
In the gorgeous turrets of Notre Dame;
But thy sounds were sweeter than the dome of Peter

Flings o'er the Tiber, pealing solemnly.
Oh! the bells of Shandon
Sound far more grand on
The pleasant waters of the river Lee.

There's a bell in Moscow, while on tower and Kiosko
In St Sophia the Turkman gets,
And loud in air calls men to prayer
From the tapering summit of tall minarets.
Such empty phantom I freely grant 'em,
But there's an anthem more dear to me:
'Tis the bells of Shandon,
That sound so grand on
The pleasant waters of the river Lee.

Father Prout

Bad Luck to this Marching

Bad luck to this marching,
Pipeclaying and starching
How neat one must be to be killed by the French!
I'm sick of parading,
Through wet and cold wading,
Or standing all night to be shot in a trench.
To the tune of a fife
They dispose of your life,
You surrender your soul to some illigant lilt;
Now I like 'Garryowen'
When I hear it at home,
But it's not half so sweet when you're going to be kilt.

Then, though up late and early
Our pay comes so rarely,
The devil a farthing we've ever to spare;
They say some disaster
Befell the paymaster;
On my conscience I think that the money's not there.

And, just think, what a blunder,
They won't let us plunder,
While the convents invite us to rob them, 'tis clear;
Though there isn't a village
But cries, 'Come and pillage!'
Yet we leave all the mutton behind for Mounseer.

Like a sailor that's nigh land,
I long for that island
Where even the kisses we steal if we please;
Where it is no disgrace
If you don't wash your face,
And you've nothing to do but to stand at your ease.
With no sergeant to abuse us,
We fight to amuse us,
Sure it's better beat Christians than kick a baboon;
How I'd dance like a fairy
To see ould Dunleary,
And think twice ere I'd leave it to be a dragoon!

Charles James Lever

Lament for the Death of Thomas Davis

I walked through Ballinderry in the springtime,
When the bud was on the tree,
And I said, in every fresh-ploughed field beholding
The sowers striding free,
Scattering broadcast forth the corn in golden plenty,
On the quick, seed-clasping soil,
'Even such this day among the fresh-stirred hearts of Erin,
Thomas Davis, is thy toil!'

I sat by Ballyshannon in the summer,
And saw the salmon leap,
And I said, as I beheld the gallant creatures

Spring glittering from the deep,
'Through the spray and through the prone heaps striving
    onward
To the calm clear streams above,
So seekest thou thy native founts of freedom, Thomas Davis,
In thy brightness of strength and love!'

I stood on Derrybawn in the autumn,
I heard the eagle call,
With a clangorous cry of wrath and lamentation
That filled the wide mountain hall,
O'er the bare, deserted place of his plundered eyrie,
And I said, as he screamed and soared,
'So callest thou, thou wrathful-soaring Thomas Davis,
For a nation's rights restored.'

And alas! to think but now that thou art lying,
Dear Davis, dead at thy mother's knee,
And I, no mother near, on my own sick-bed,
That face on earth shall never see.
I may lie and try to feel that I am not dreaming,
I may lie and try to say, 'Thy Will be done' –
But a hundred such as I will not comfort Erin
For the loss of that noble son.

Young husbandman of Erin's faithful seed-time,
In the fresh track of danger's plough!
Who will walk the heavy, toilsome, perilous furrow,
Girt with freedom's seed-sheets now?
Who will vanish with the wholesome crop of knowledge,
The flaunting weed and the bitter thorn,
Now that thou thyself art but a seed for hopeful planting
Against the resurrection morn?

Young salmon of the flood-time of freedom
That swells round Erin's shore,
Thou wilt leap against their loud, oppressive torrents
Of bigotry and hate no more!
Drawn downward by their prone material instinct,

137

Let them thunder on their rocks, and foam;
Thou hast leaped, aspiring soul, to founts beyond their
      raging,
Where troubled waters never come.

But I grieve not, eagle of the empty eyrie,
That thy wrathful cry is still,
And that the songs alone of peaceful mourners
Are heard today on Erin's hill.
Better far if brothers' war be destined for us –
God avert that horrid day, I pray! –
That ere our hands be stained with slaughter fratricidal,
Thy warm heart should be cold in clay.

But my trust is strong in God who made us brothers,
That He will not suffer these right hands,
Which thou hast joined in holier rites than wedlock,
To draw opposing brands.
O many a tuneful tongue that thou madest vocal,
Would lie cold and silent then,
And songless long once more should often-widowed Erin,
Mourn the loss of her brave young men.

O brave young men, my love, my pride, my promise,
'Tis on you my hopes are set,
In manliness, in kindliness, in justice,
To make Erin a nation yet;
Self-respecting, self-relying, self-advancing,
In union or in severance, free and strong,
And if God grant this, then, under God, to Thomas Davis,
Let the greater praise belong!

Samuel Ferguson

The Battle Eve of the Brigade

After the flight of the earls, O'Neill and O'Donnell in 1607, numbers of Irish crowded into all the Continental services (Spain, France, Austria and Italy). Many of the Irish who had had their fortunes taken by Cromwell served in the foreign armies. Throughout the years the number of Irishmen in foreign service increased particularly at the time of the Jacobite wars. Sarsfield and the remnants of his army went to France – one of the most dramatic scenes in Irish history. The heroic deeds of the officers and men of the various Irish battalions have been a fertile source of inspiration for the poets of Ireland. The recruiting for the Brigade was carried on in the French ships which smuggled brandies, wines, silks, etc., to the western and south-western coasts. Their return cargoes were recruits for the Brigade, and were entered in their books as Wild Geese. Hence this became the common name in Ireland for the Irish serving in the Brigade. The recruitment was chiefly in Clare, Limerick, Cork, Kerry and Galway.

The mess-tent is full, and the glasses are set,
And the gallant Count Thomond is president yet;
The vet'ran arose, like an uplifted lance,
Crying – 'Comrades, a health to the monarch of France!'
With bumpers and cheers they have done as he bade,
For King Louis is loved by The Irish Brigade.

'A health to King James,' and they bent as they quaffed;
'Here's to George the *Elector*,' and fiercely they laughed;
'Good luck to the girls we wooed long ago,
Where Shannon, and Barrow, and Blackwater flow;'
'God prosper old Ireland,' – you'd think them afraid,
So pale grew the chiefs of The Irish Brigade.

'But surely, that light cannot come from our lamp?
And the noise – are they *all* getting drunk in the camp?'
'Hurrah! boys, the morning of battle is come,
And the *generale's* beating on many a drum.'
So they rush from the revel to join the parade;
For the van is the right of The Irish Brigade.

They fought as they revelled, fast, fiery and true,
And, though victors, they left on the field not a few;
And they, who survived, fought and drank as of yore,
But the land of their heart's hope they never saw more;
For in far foreign fields, from Dunkirk to Belgrade,
Lie the soldiers and chiefs of The Irish Brigade.

Thomas Davis

The Little Black Rose

The Little Black Rose[1] shall be red at last;
What made it black but the March wind dry,
And the tear of the widow that fell on it fast?
It shall redden the hills when June is nigh.

The Silk of the Kine shall rest at last;
What drove her forth but the dragon-fly?
In the golden vale she shall feed full fast,
With her mild gold horn and slow, dark eye.

The wounded wood-dove lies dead at last!
The pine long bleeding, it shall not die!
This song is secret. Mine ear is passed
In a wind o'er the plains at Athenry.

Aubrey de Vere

Galway Races

It's there you'll see confectioners with sugar-sticks and
      dainties,
The lozenges and oranges, the lemonade and raisins;
The gingerbread and spices to accommodate the ladies,
And a big crubeen for threepence to be picking while you're
      able.

It's there you'll see the gamblers, the thimbles and the
      garters,
And the sporting wheel of fortune with the four and twenty
      quarters.
There was others without scruple pelting wattles at poor
      Maggy,
And her father well contented and he looking at his
      daughter.

---

[1] *Little Black Rose, and Silk of the Kine are mystical names for Ireland.*

140

It's there you'll see the pipers and fiddlers competing,
And the nimble-footed dancers and they tripping on the
     daisies.
There was others crying segars and lights, and bills of all the
     races,
With the colour of the jockeys, the prize and horses' ages.

It's there you'd see the jockeys and they mounted on most
     stately,
The pink and blue, the red and green, the emblem of our
     nation.
When the bell was rung for starting, the horses seemed
     impatient,
Though they never stood on ground, their speed was so
     amazing.

There was half a million people there of all denominations,
The Catholic, the Protestant, the Jew and Prespetarian.
There was yet no animosity, no matter what persuasion,
But *fáilte* and hospitality, including fresh acquaintance.

                                     Anonymous

The Man from God-Knows-Where

Into our townlan', on a night of snow,
Rode a man from God-knows-where;
None of us bade him stay or go,
Nor deemed him friend, nor damned him foe,
But we stabled his big roan mare:
For in our townlan' we're decent folk,
And if he didn't speak, why none of us spoke,
And we sat till the fire burned low.

We're a civil sort in our wee place,
So we made the circle wide
Round Andy Lemon's cheerful blaze,
And wished the man his length of days,

And a good end to his ride.
He smiled in under his slouchy hat –
Says he: 'There's a bit of a joke in that,
For we ride in different ways.'

The whiles we smoked we watched him stare
From his seat fornenst the glow.
I nudged Joe Moore: 'You wouldn't dare
To ask him, who he's for meeting there,
And how far he has got to go.'
But Joe wouldn't dare, nor Wully Scott,
And he took no drink – neither cold nor hot –
This man from God-knows-where.

It was closin' time, an' late for bye,
When us ones braved the air –
I never saw worse (may I live or die)
Then the sleet that night, an' I says, says I:
'You'll find he's for stopping there.'
But at screek o' day, through the gable pane,
I watched him spur in the peltin' rain
And I juked from his rovin' eye.

Two winters more, then the Trouble Year,
When the best that a man can feel
Was the pike he kept in hidin' near,
Till the blood o' hate an' the blood o' fear
Would be redder nor rust on the steel.
Us ones quiet from mindin' the farms,
Let them take what we gave wi' the weight o' our arms
From Saintfield to Kilkeel.

In the time o' the Hurry, we had no lead –
We all of us fought with the rest –
An' if e'er a one shook like a tremblin' reed,
None of us gave neither hint nor heed.
Nor ever even'd we'd guessed.
We men of the north had a word to say,
An' we said it then, in our own dour way,

An' we spoke as we thought was best.

All Ulster over, the weemen cried
For the stan'-in' crops on the lan' –
Many's the sweetheart an' many's the bride
Would liefer ha' gone till where He died,
An ha' mourned her lone by her man.
But us ones weathered the thick of it,
And we used to dander along, and sit,
In Andy's, side by side.

What with discoorse goin' to and fro,
The night would be wearin' thin,
Yet never so late when we rose to go
But someone would say: 'Do ye min' thon snow,
An' the man who came wanderin' in?'
And we be to fall the talk again,
If by any chance he was one o' them –
The man who went like the win'.

Well 'twas gettin' on past the heat o' the year
When I rode to Newtown fair:
I sold as I could the dealers were near –
Only three pounds eight for the Innish steer,
(An' nothin' at all for the mare!)
I met with M'Kee in the thong o' the street,
Says he: 'The grass has grown under our feet
Since they hanged young Warwick here.'

And he told me that Boney had promised help
To a man in Dublin town.
Says he: 'If ye've laid the pike on the shelf,
Ye'd better go home hot-fut by yerself,
An' once more take it down.'
So by Comber road I trotted the grey
And never cut corn until Killyleagh
Stood plain on the rising groun'.

For a wheen o' days we sat waitin' the word

To rise and go at it like men.
But no French ships sailed into Cloughey Bay,
And we heard the black news on a harvest day
That the cause was lost again;
And Joey and me, and Wully Boy Scott,
We agreed to ourselves we'd lief as not
Ha' been found in the thick o' the slain.

By Downpatrick gaol I was bound to fare
On a day I'll remember, feth,
For when I came to the prison square
The people were waitin' in hundreds there,
An' you wouldn't hear stir nor breath!
For the sodgers were standing, grim an' tall,
Round a scaffold built there fornent the wall.
An' a man stepped out for death!

I was brave an' near to the edge of the throng,
Yet I knowed the face again.
An' I knowed the set, an' I knowed the walk
An' the sound of his strange up-country talk,
For he spoke out right an' plain.
Then he bowed his head to the swinging rope,
Whiles I said 'Please God' to his dying hope
And 'Amen' to his dying prayer,
That the wrong would cease and the right prevail,
For the man that they hanged at Downpatrick Gaol
Was the Man from GOD-KNOWS-WHERE!

Florence Wilson

The Rose of Tralee

The pale moon was rising above the green mountain,
The sun was declining beneath the blue sea,
When I stray'd with my love to the pure crystal fountain
That stands in the beautiful vale of Tralee.

She was lovely and fair as the rose of the summer,
Yet 'twas not her beauty alone that won me,
Oh no, 'twas the truth in her eyes ever beaming
That made me love Mary, the Rose of Tralee.

The cool shades of evening their mantle were spreading,
And Mary, all smiling, was list'ning to me,
The moon through the valley her pale rays was shedding
When I won the heart of the Rose of Tralee.

Tho' lovely and fair as the rose of the summer,
Yet 'twas not her beauty alone that won me,
Oh, no, 'twas the truth in her eyes ever beaming
That made me love Mary, the Rose of Tralee.

William Pembroke Mulchinock

The Dying Girl

From a Munster vale they brought her,
From the pure and balmy air;
An Ormond peasant's daughter,
With blue eyes and golden hair.
They brought her to the city
And she faded slowly there –
Consumption has no pity
For blue eyes and golden hair.

When I saw her first reclining
Her lips were mov'd in prayer,
And the setting sun was shining
On her loosen'd golden hair.
When our kindly glances met her,
Deadly brilliant was her eye;
And she said that she was better,
While we knew that she must die.

She speaks of Munster valleys,

The pattern, dance and fair,
And her thin hand feebly dallies
With her scattered golden hair.
When silently we listen'd
To her breath with quiet care,
Her eyes with wonder glisten'd,
And she asked us, 'What was there?'

The poor thing smiled to ask it,
And her pretty mouth laid bare,
Like gems within a casket,
A string of pearlets rare.
We said that we were trying
By the gushing of her blood
And the time she took in sighing
To know if she were good.

Well, she smil'd and chatted gaily,
Though we saw in mute despair
The hectic brighter daily,
And the death-dew on her hair.
And oft her wasted fingers
Beating time upon the bed:
O'er some old tune she lingers,
And she bows her golden head.

At length the harp is broken;
And the spirit in its strings,
As the last decree is spoken,
To its source exulting springs.
Descending swiftly from the skies
Her guardian angel came,
He struck God's lightning from her eyes,
And bore Him back the flame.

Before the sun had risen
Through the lark-loved morning air,
Her young soul left its prison,
Undefiled by sin or care.

I stood beside the couch in tears
Where pale and calm she slept,
And though I've gazed on death for years,
I blush not that I wept.

I check'd with effort pity's sighs
And left the matron there,
To close the curtains to her eyes
And bind her golden hair.

Richard D'Alton Williams

The Coolun

O had you seen the Coolun,
Walking down the cuckoo's street,
With the dew of the meadow shining
On her milk-white twinkling feet!
My love she is, and my coleen oge,
And she dwells in Bal'nagar;
And she bears the palm of beauty bright,
From the fairest that in Erin are.

In Bal'nagar is the Coolun,
Like the berry on the bough her cheek;
Bright beauty dwells for ever
On her fair neck and ringlets sleek;
Oh, sweeter is her mouth's soft music
Than the lark or thrush at dawn,
Or the blackbird in the greenwood singing
Farewell to the setting sun.

Rise up, my boy! make ready
My horse, for I forth would ride,
To follow the modest damsel,
Where she walks on the green hillside:
For ever since our youth were we plighted,
In faith, troth, and wedlock true –
She is sweeter to me nine times over,

Than organ or cuckoo!

For, ever since my childhood
I loved the fair and darling child;
But our people came between us,
And with lucre our pure love defiled:
Ah, my woe it is, and my bitter pain,
And I weep it night and day,
That the coleen bawn of my early love
Is torn from my heart away.

Sweetheart and faithful treasure
Be constant, still and true;
Nor for want of herds and houses
Leave one who would ne'er leave you.
I'll pledge you the blessed Bible,
Without and eke within,
That the faithful God will provide for us,
Without thanks to kith or kin.

Oh, love, do you remember
When we lay all night alone,
Beneath the ash in the winter storm,
When the oak wood round did groan?
No shelter then from the blast had we,
The bitter blast or sleet,
But your gown to wrap about our heads,
And my coat around our feet.

Maurice O'Dugan – Translated by Samuel Ferguson

The Redemptorist

'How many children have you?' asked
The big Redemptorist.
'Six, Father.'
'The last,
When was it born?'

148

'Ten months ago.'
'I cannot absolve your mortal sin
Until you conceive again. Go home,
Obey your husband.'
She whimpered:
'But
The doctor warned me ...'
Shutter became
Her coffin lid. She twisted her thin hands
And left the box.
The missioner,
Red-bearded saint, had brought hell's flame
To frighten women on retreat:
Sent on his spiritual errand,
It rolled along the village street
Until Rathfarnham was housing smoke
That sooted the Jesuits in their castle.
'No pregnancy. You'll die the next time,'
The doctor had said.
Her tiredness obeyed
That Saturday night:
Her husband's weight
Digging her grave. So, in nine months, she
Sank in great agony on a Monday.
Her children wept in the orphanage,
Huddled together in the annexe,
While, proud of the Black Cross on his badge,
The Liguorian, at Adam and Eve's,
Ascended the pulpit, sulphuring his sleeves
And setting fire to the holy text.

Austin Clarke

First Autumn Night
(for Martin)

In the first Autumn night
I open my window,

149

looking for your flame
to roar into me
from beyond the moon's
pearl-cool gaze.

My nostrils reach
for your smell
from the leaf-damp air,
your white, flaring laugh
from the mottled rustlings
in the eaves,
but the night toad squats, unmoved,
his fat throat
flickers dark green,
he has swallowed the sun.
His dank hide
eclipses your face,
the trees sweep you away
with their weary arms
like the last of summer.

I turn in
to my doll-yellow room,
where pieces of you dart
unfinished and awry –
your head a sunflower,
(blue birds, your eyes),
your firefingers on my skin,
the hot caprice of your tongue,
the eager blaze of your sex,
your long thigh
ember warm on mine –

I pull you around me
like a golden skin,
like a patched blanket
in the first Autumn chill.

Katie Donovan

Dark Rosaleen

O, my Dark Rosaleen,
Do not sigh, do not weep!
The priests are on the ocean green,
They march along the Deep.
There's wine ... from the royal pope,
Upon the ocean green;
And Spanish ale shall give you hope,
My Dark Rosaleen!
My own Rosaleen!
Shall glad your heart, shall give you hope,
Shall give you health, and help, and hope,
My Dark Rosaleen!

Over hills, and through dales,
Have I roamed for your sake;
All yesterday I sailed with sails
On river and on lake.
The Erne ... at its highest flood,
I dashed across unseen,
For there was lightning in my blood,
My Dark Rosaleen!
My own Rosaleen!
Oh! there was lightning in my blood,
Red lightning lightened through my blood,
My Dark Rosaleen!

All day long, in unrest,
To and fro, do I move.
The very soul within my breast
Is wasted for you, love!
The heart ... in my bosom faints
To think of you, my Queen,
My life of life, my saint of saints,
My Dark Rosaleen!

My own Rosaleen!
To hear your sweet and sad complaints,
My life, my love, my saint of saints,
My Dark Rosaleen!

Woe and pain, pain and woe,
Are my lot, night and noon,
To see your bright face clouded so,
Like to the mournful moon.
But yet ... will I rear your throne
Again in golden sheen;
'Tis you shall reign, shall reign alone,
My Dark Rosaleen!
My own Rosaleen!
'Tis you shall have the golden throne,
'Tis you shall reign, and reign alone,
My Dark Rosaleen!

Over dews, over sands,
Will I fly, for your weal:
Your holy delicate white hands
Shall girdle me with steel
At home ... in your emerald bowers,
From morning's dawn till e'en,
You'll pray for me, my flower of flowers,
My Dark Rosaleen!
My fond Rosaleen!
You'll think of me through Daylight's hours,
My virgin flower, my flower of flowers,
My Dark Rosaleen!

I could scale the blue air,
I could plough the high hills,
Oh, I could kneel all night in prayer,
To heal your many ills!
And one ... beamy smile from you
Would float like light between
My toils and me, my own, my true,
My Dark Rosaleen!

My fond Rosaleen!
Would give me life and soul anew,
A second life, a soul anew,
My Dark Rosaleen!

O! the Erne shall run red
With redundance of blood,
The earth shall rock beneath our tread,
And flames wrap hill and wood,
And gun-peal, and slogan cry,
Wake many a glen serene.
Ere you shall fade, ere you shall die,
My Dark Rosaleen!
My own Rosaleen!
The Judgment Hour must first be nigh,
Ere you can fade, ere you can die,
My Dark Rosaleen!

Owen Roe MacWard – Translated by James Clarence Mangan

To the Oaks of Glencree

My arms are round you, and I lean
Against you, while the lark
Sings over us, and golden lights, and green
Shadows are on your bark.

There'll come a season when you'll stretch
Black boards to cover me:
Then in Mount Jerome I will lie, poor wretch,
With worms eternally.

J M Synge

A Question

I asked if I got sick and died, would you

With my black funeral go walking too.
If you'd stand close to hear them talk or pray
While I'm let down in that steep bank of clay.

And, No, you said, for if you saw a crew
Of living idiots pressing round that new
Oak coffin – they alive, I dead beneath
That board – you'd rave and rend them with your teeth.

J M Synge

A Dream

I heard the dogs howl in the moonlight night;
I went to the window to see the sight;
All the Dead that ever I knew
Going one by one and two by two.

On they pass'd, and on they pass'd;
Townsfellows all, from first to last;
Born in the moonlight of the lane,
Quench'd in the heavy shadow again.

Schoolmates marching as when we play'd
At soldiers once – but now more staid;
Those were the strangest sight to me
Who were drown'd, I knew, in the awful sea.

Straight and handsome folk; bent and weak, too;
Some that I loved, and gasp'd to speak to;
Some but a day in their churchyard bed;
Some that I had not known were dead.

A long, long crowd – where each seem'd lonely,
Yet of them all there was one, one only,
Raised a head or look'd my way:
She linger'd a moment – she might not stay.

How long since I saw that fair pale face!
Ah! Mother dear! might I only place

My head on thy breast, a moment to rest,
While thy hand on my tearful cheek were prest!

On, on, a moving bridge they made
Across the moon-stream, from shade to shade,
Young and old, women and men;
Many long-forgot, but remember'd then.

William Allingham

Lovely Mary Donnelly

Oh, lovely Mary Donnelly, my joy, my only best!
If fifty girls were round you, I'd hardly see the rest;
Be what it may the time o' day, the place be where it will,
Sweet looks o' Mary Donnelly, they bloom before me still.

Her eyes like mountain water that's flowing on a rock,
How clear they are, how dark they are! they give me many a
      shock;
Red rowans warm in sunshine and wetted with a show'r,
Could ne'er express the charming lip that has me in its
      pow'r.

Her nose is straight and handsome, her eye-brows lifted up,
Her chin is very neat and pert, and smooth like a china cup,
Her hair's the brag of Ireland, so weighty and so fine;
It's rolling down upon her neck, and gather'd in a twine.

The dance o' last Whit-Monday night exceeded all before,
No pretty girl for miles about was missing from the floor;
But Mary kept the belt o' love, and oh, but she was gay!
She danced a jig, she sung a song, that took my heart away.

When she stood up for dancing, her steps were so complete
The music nearly kill'd itself to listen to her feet;
The fiddler moan'd his blindness, he heard her so much
      praised,

But bless'd his luck to not be deaf when once her voice she
      raised.

And evermore I'm whistling or lilting what you sung,
Your smile is always in my heart, your name beside my
      tongue;
But you've as many sweethearts as you'd count on both
      your hands,
And for myself there's not a thumb or little finger stands.

'Tis you're the flower o' womankind in country or in town;
The higher I exalt you, the lower I'm cast down.
If some great lord should come this way, and see your
      beauty bright,
And you to be his lady, I'd own it was but right.

Oh, might we live together in a lofty palace hall,
Where joyful music rises, and where scarlet curtains fall!
Oh, might we live together in a cottage mean and small,
With sods o' grass the only roof and mud the only wall!

Oh, lovely Mary Donnelly, your beauty's my distress,
It's far too beauteous to be mine, but I'll never wish it less.
The proudest place would fit your face, and I am poor and
      low;
But blessings be about you, dear, wherever you may go!

William Allingham

The Jewish Bride

(After Rembrandt)

At the black canvas of estrangement,
As the smoke empties from the ruins under a gold
  Winter sky,
Death-trains clattering across the back gardens of
  Amsterdam
– Sheds, buckets, wire, concrete
– Manholes, pumps, pliers, scaffolding:

I see, as if for the first time,
The person you were, and are, and always will be
Despite the evil that men do:
The teenage girl on the brink of womanhood
Who, when I met you, was on the brink of everything –
Composing fairytales and making drawings
That used to remind your friends of Anderson and
    Thurber –
Living your hidden life that promised everything
Despite all the maimed, unreliable men and women
Who were at that moment congregating all around you:
Including, of course, most of all, myself.
You made of your bedroom a flowing stream
Into which, daily, you threw proofs of your dreams;
Pinned to your bedroom wall with brass-studded
    drawing pins
Newspaper and magazine photographs of your heroes
    and heroines,
People who met you breathed the air of freedom,
And sensuality fragile as it was wild:
'Nessa's air makes free' people used to say,
Like in the dark ages, 'Town air makes free'.
The miracle is that you survived me.
You stroll about the malls and alleyways of Amsterdam,
About its islands and bridges, its archways and jetties,
With Spring in your heels, although it is Winter;
Privately, publicly, along the Grand Parade;
A Jewish Bride who has survived the death-camp,
Free at last of my swastika eyes
Staring at you from across spiked dinner plates
Or from out of the bunker of a TV armchair;
Free of the glare off my jackboot silence;
Free of the hysteria of my gestapo voice;
Now your shyness replenished with all your old cheeky
    confidence –
That grassy well at which red horses used to rear up and
    sip
With young men naked riding bareback calling your
    name.

Dog-muzzle of tension torn down from your face;
Black polythene of asphyxiation peeled away from your
   soul;
Your green eyes quivering with dark, sunny laughter
And – all spread-eagled and supple again – your loving,
   freckled hands.

Paul Durcan

The Man of the North Countrie

He came from the North and his words were few,
But his voice was kind and his heart was true;
And I knew by his eyes no guile had he,
So I married the man of the North Countrie.

Oh! Garryowen may be more gay,
Than this quiet street of Ballibay;
And I know the sun shines softly down
On the river that passes my native town.

But there's not – I say it with joy and pride –
Better man than mine in Munster wide;
And Limerick town has no happier hearth
Than mine has been with my man of the North.

I wish that in Munster they only knew
The kind, kind neighbours I came unto:
Small hate or scorn would ever be
Between the South and North countrie.

Thomas D'Arcy M'Gee

Like Dolmens Round my Childhood, the Old People

Like dolmens round my childhood, the old people.

Jamie MacCrystal sang to himself,

A broken song without tune, without words;
He tipped me a penny every pension day,
Fed kindly crusts to winter birds.
When he died, his cottage was robbed,
Mattress and money box torn and searched.
Only the corpse they didn't disturb.

Maggie Owens was surrounded by animals,
A mongrel bitch and shivering pups,
Even in her bedroom a she-goat cried.
She was a well of gossip defiled,
Fanged chronicler of a whole countryside:
Reputed a witch, all I could find
Was her lonely need to deride.

The Nialls lived along a mountain lane
Where heather bells bloomed, clumps of foxglove.
All were blind, with Blind Pension and Wireless,
Dead eyes serpent-flicked as one entered
To shelter from a downpour of mountain rain.
Crickets chirped under the rocking hearthstone
Until the muddy sun shone out again.

Mary Moore lived in a crumbling gatehouse,
Famous as Pisa for its leaning gable.
Bag-apron and boots, she tramped the fields
Driving lean cattle from a miry stable.
A by-word for fierceness, she fell asleep
Over love stories, Red Star and Red Circle,
Dreamed of gypsy love rites, by firelight sealed.

Wild Billy Eagleson married a Catholic serving girl
When all his Loyal family passed on:
We danced round him shouting, 'To hell with king
    Billy,'
And dodged from the arc of his flailing blackthorn.
Forsaken by both creeds, he showed little concern
Until the Orange drums banged past in the summer
And bowler and sash aggressively shone.

Curate and doctor trudged to attend them,
Through knee-deep snow, through summer heat,
From main road to lane to broken path,
Gulping the mountain air with painful breath.
Sometimes they were found by neighbours,
Silent keepers of a smokeless hearth,
Suddenly cast in the mould of death.

Ancient Ireland, indeed! I was reared by her bedside,
The rune and the chant, evil eye and averted head,
Fomorian fierceness of family and local feud.
Gaunt figures of fear and of friendliness,
For years they trespassed on my dreams,
Until once, in a standing circle of stones,
I felt their shadows pass

Into that dark permanence of ancient forms.

John Montague

Ode

We are the music-makers,
And we are the dreamers of dreams,
Wandering by lone sea-breakers,
And sitting by desolate streams; –

World-losers and world-forsakers,
On whom the pale moon gleams:
Yet we are the movers and shakers
Of the world for ever, it seems.

With wonderful deathless ditties
We build up the world's great cities,
And out of a fabulous story
We fashion an empire's glory:

One man with a dream, at pleasure,
Shall go forth and conquer a crown;

And three with a new song's measure
Can trample an empire down.

We, in the ages lying
In the buried past of the earth,
Built Nineveh with our sighing,
And Babel itself with our mirth;
And o'erthrew them with prophesying
To the old of the new world's worth;
For each age is a dream that is dying,
Or one that is coming to birth.

Arthur O'Shaughnessy

A Disused Shed in Co. Wexford
For J G Farrell

Let them not forget us, the weak souls among the asphodels.
– Seferis, Mythistorema, *tr Keeley and Sherrard*

Even now there are places where a thought might grow –
Peruvian mines, worked out and abandoned
To a slow clock of condensation,
An echo trapped for ever, and a flutter
Of wild-flowers in the lift-shaft,
Indian compounds where the wind dances
And a door bangs with diminished confidence,
Lime crevices behind rippling rain-barrels,
Dog corners for bone burials;
And in a disused shed in Co. Wexford,

Deep in the grounds of a burnt-out hotel,
Among the bathtubs and the washbasins
A thousand mushrooms crowd to a keyhole.
This is the one star in their firmament
Or frames a star within a star.
What should they do there but desire?
So many days beyond the rhododendrons
With the world waltzing in its bowl of cloud,
They have learnt patience and silence

161

Listening to the rooks querulous in the high wood.

They have been waiting for us in a foetor
Of vegetable sweat since civil war days,
Since the gravel-crunching, interminable departure
Of the expropriated mycologist.
He never came back, and light since then
Is a keyhole rusting gently after rain.
Spiders have spun, flies dusted to mildew
And once a day, perhaps, they have heard something –
A trickle of masonry, a shout from the blue
Or a lorry changing gear at the end of the lane.

There have been deaths, the pale flesh flaking
Into the earth that nourished it;
And nightmares, born of these and the grim
Dominion of stale air and rank moisture.
Those nearest the door grow strong –
'Elbow room! Elbow room!'
The rest, dim in a twilight of crumbling
Utensils and broken pitchers, groaning
For their deliverance, have been so long
Expectant that there is left only the posture.

A half century, without visitors, in the dark –
Poor preparation for the cracking lock
And creak of hinges. Magi, moonmen,
Powdery prisoners of the old regime,
Web-throated, stalked like triffids, racked by drought
And insomnia, only the ghost of a scream
At the flash-bulb firing-squad we wake them with
Shows there is life yet in their feverish forms.
Grown beyond nature now, soft food for worms,
They lift frail heads in gravity and good faith.

They are begging us, you see, in their wordless way,
To do something, to speak on their behalf
Or at least not to close the door again.
Lost people of Treblinka and Pompeii!
'Save us, save us,' they seem to say,

'Let the god not abandon us
Who have come so far in darkness and in pain.
We too had our lives to live.
You with your light meter and relaxed itinerary,
Let not our naive labours have been in vain!'

Derek Mahon

An Ulsterman

I do not like the other sort;
They're tricky an' they're sly,
An' couldn't look you in the face
Whenever they pass by.
Still I'll give in that here an' there,
You'll meet a decent man;
I would make an exception, now,
About wee Michael Dan.

But, then, he's from about the doors,
An' lived here all his days,
An' mixin' with us in an' out,
He's fell into our ways.
He pays his debts an' keeps his word
An' does the best he can.
If only all the Papishes
Were like wee Michael Dan!

A better neighbour couldn't be.
He borrows an' he lends;
An' – bar a while about the Twelfth
When him an' me's not friends –
He'll never wait until he's asked
To lend a helpin' han'.
There's quite a wheen of Protestants
I'd swop for Michael Dan.

Of course he'd burn me at the stake,

163

I know that very well;
An' told me one day to my face
I'm not too safe from hell.
But when I backed a bill for him
He met it like a man.
There's sparks of Christianity
About wee Michael Dan.

So, while I have my private doubts
About him reachin' heaven,
His feet keeps purty near the pad
On six days out of seven;
An' if it falls within the scope
Of God Almighty's plan
To save a single Papish sowl,
I hope it's Michael Dan.

Lynn Doyle

John-John

I dreamt last night of you, John-John,
And thought you called to me;
And when I woke this morning, John,
Yourself I hoped to see;
But I was all alone, John-John,
Though still I heard your call:
I put my boots and bonnet on,
And took my Sunday shawl.
And went, full sure to find you, John,
To Nenagh fair.

The fair was just the same as then,
Five years ago today,
When first you left the thimble men
And came with me away;
For there again were thimble men
And shooting galleries,

And card-trick men and Maggie men
Of all sorts and degrees –
But not a sight of you, John-John,
Was anywhere.

I turned my face to home again,
And called myself a fool
To think you'd leave the thimble men
And live again by rule,
And go to mass and keep the fast
And till the little patch:
My wish to have you home was past
Before I raised the latch
And pushed the door and saw you, John,
Sitting down there.

How cool you came in here, begad,
As if you owned the place!
But rest yourself there now, my lad,
'Tis good to see your face;
My dream is out, and now by it
I think I know my mind:
At six o'clock this house you'll quit,
And leave no grief behind; –
But until six o'clock, John-John,
My bit you'll share.

My neighbours' shame of me began
When first I brought you in;
To wed and keep a tinker man
They thought a kind of sin;
But now this three year since you're gone
'Tis pity me they do,
And that I'd rather have John-John,
Than that they'd pity you.
Pity for me and you, John-John,
I could not bear.

Oh, you're my husband right enough,
But what's the good of that?

You know you never were the stuff
To be the cottage cat,
To watch the fire and hear me lock
The door and put out Shep –
But there now, it is six o'clock
And time for you to step.
God bless and keep you far, John-John!
And that's my prayer.

Thomas MacDonagh

Ulster Names

I take my stand by the Ulster names,
each clean hard name like a weathered stone;
Tyrella, Rostrevor, are flickering flames:
the names I mean are the Moy, Malone,
Strabane, Slieve Gullion and Portglenone.

Even suppose that each name were freed
from legend's ivy and history's moss,
there'd be music still, in say, Carrick-a-rede,
though men forget it's the rock across
the track of the salmon from Islay and Ross.

The names of a land show the heart of the race;
they move on the tongue like the lilt of a song.
You say the name and I see the place –
Drumbo, Dungannon, or Annalong.
Barony, townland, we cannot go wrong.

You say Armagh, and I see the hill
with the two tall spires or the square low tower;
the faith of Patrick is with us still;
his blessing falls in a moonlit hour,
when the apple orchards are all in flower.

You whisper Derry. Beyond the walls
and the crashing boom and the coiling smoke,

I follow that freedom which beckons and calls
to Colmcille tall in his grove of oak,
raising his voice for the rhyming folk.

County by county you number them over;
Tyrone, Fermanagh ... I stand by a lake,
and the bubbling curlew, the whistling plover
call over the whins in the chill daybreak
as the hills and the waters the first light take.

Let Down be famous for care-tilled earth,
for the little green hills and the harsh grey peaks,
the rocky bed of the Lagan's birth,
the white farm fat in the August weeks.
There's one more county my pride still seeks.

You give it the name and my quick thoughts run
through the narrow towns with their wheels of trade,
to Glenballyemon, Glenaan, Glendun,
from Trostan down to the braes of Layde
for there is the place where the pact was made.

But you have as good a right as I
To praise the place where your face is known,
for over us all is the selfsame sky;
the limestone's locked in the strength of the bone
and who shall mock at the steadfast stone?

So it's Ballinamallard, it's Crossmaglen,
It's Aughnacloy, it's Donaghadee,
It's Magherafelt breeds the best of men
I'll not deny it. But look for me
on the moss between Orra and Slievenanee.

John Hewitt

The Man Upright

I once spent an evening in a village

Where the people are all taken up with tillage,
Or do some business in a small way
Among themselves, and all the day
Go crooked, doubled to half their size,
Both working and loafing, with their eyes
Stuck in the ground or in a board, –
For some of them tailor, and some of them hoard
Pence in a till in their little shops,
And some of them shoe-soles – they get the tops
Ready-made from England, and they die cobblers –
All bent up double, a village of hobblers
And slouchers and squatters, whether they straggle
Up and down, or bend to haggle
Over a counter, or bend at a plough,
Or to dig with a spade, or to milk a cow,
Or to shove the goose-iron stiffly along
The stuff on the sleeve-board, or lace the fong
In the boot on the last, or to draw the wax-end
Tight cross-ways – and so to make or to mend
What will soon be worn out by the crooked people.
The only thing straight in the place was the steeple,
I thought at first. I was wrong in that;
For there past the window at which I sat
Watching the crooked little men
Go slouching, and with the gait of a hen
An odd little woman go pattering past,
And the cobbler crouching over his last
In the window opposite, and next door
The tailor squatting inside on the floor –
While I watched them, as I have said before,
And thought that only the steeple was straight,
There came a man of a different gait –
A man who neither slouched nor pattered,
But planted his steps as if each step mattered;
Yet walked down the middle of the street
Not like a policeman on his beat,
But like a man with nothing to do
Except walk straight upright like me and you.

Thomas MacDonagh

Máire my Girl

Over the dim blue hills
Strays a wild river,
Over the dim blue hills
Rests my heart ever.
Dearer and brighter than
Jewels and pearl,
Dwells she in beauty there,
Máire my girl.

Down upon Claris heath
Shines the soft berry,
On the brown harvest tree
Droops the red cherry.
Sweeter thy honey lips,
Softer the curl
Straying adown thy cheeks,
Máire my girl.

'Twas on an April eve
That I first met her;
Many an eve shall pass
Ere I forget her,
Since my young heart has been
Wrapped in a whirl,
Thinking and dreaming of
Máire my girl.

She is too kind and fond
Ever to grieve me,
She has too pure a heart
E'er to deceive me.
Were I Tyrconnell's chief
Or Desmond's earl,
Life would be dark, wanting
Máire my girl.

Over the dim blue hills

Strays a wild river
Over the dim blue hills
Rests my heart ever;
Dearer and brighter than
Jewels or pearl,
Dwells she in beauty there,
Máire my girl.

John Keegan Casey

Poem
For Marie

Love, I shall perfect for you the child
Who diligently potters in my brain
Digging with heavy spade till sods were piled
Or puddling through muck in a deep drain.

Yearly I would sow my yard-long garden.
I'd strip a layer of sods to build the wall
That was to exclude sow and pecking hen.
Yearly, admitting these, the sods would fall.

Or in the sucking clabber I would splash
Delightedly and dam the flowing drain
But always my bastions of clay and mush
Would burst before the rising autumn rain.

Love, you shall perfect for me this child
Whose small imperfect limits would keep breaking:
Within new limits now, arrange the world
Within our walls, within our golden ring.

Seamus Heaney

Dread

Beside a chapel I'd a room looked down,

Where all the women from the farms and town,
On Holy-days, and Sundays used to pass
To marriages, and Christenings and to Mass.

Then I sat lonely watching score and score,
Till I turned jealous of the Lord next door ...
Now by this window, where there's none can see,
The Lord God's jealous of yourself and me.

J M Synge

The Orange Lily-o

Oh did you go to see the show,
Each rose an pink a dilly-o,
To feast your eyes upon the prize,
Won by the Orange Lily-o.
The viceroy there so debonair,
Just like a daffy dilly-o
And Lady Clarke, blithe as a lark,
Approached the Orange Lily-o.

Chorus

Then heigh-o the Lily-o,
The royal, loyal Lily-o.
Beneath the sky what flower can vie,
With Ireland's Orange Lily-o.

The elated muse, to hear the news,
Jumped like a Connaught filly-o,
As gossip fame did loud proclaim
The triumph of the Lily-o;
The lowland field may roses yield,
Gay heaths the highlands hilly-o,
But high or low, no flower can show,
Like the glorious Orange Lily-o.

Then heigh-o the Lily-o,
The royal, loyal Lily-o.

There's not a flower in Erin's bower
Can match the Orange Lily-o.

Anonymous

The Croppy Boy
(A Ballad of 1798)

'Good men and true! in this house who dwell,
To a stranger bouchal, I pray you tell
Is the priest at home? or may he be seen?
I would speak a word with Father Green.'

'The priest's at home, boy, and may be seen;
'Tis easy speaking with Father Green;
But you must wait, till I go and see
If the holy father alone may be.'

The youth has entered an empty hall –
What a lonely sound has his light foot-fall!
And the gloomy chamber's chill and bare,
With a vested Priest in a lonely chair.

The youth has knelt to tell his sins;
'Nomine Dei,' the youth begins:
At 'mea culpa' he beats his breast,
And in broken murmurs he speaks the rest.

'At the siege of Ross did my father fall,
And at Gorey my loving brothers all,
I alone am left of my name and race,
I will go to Wexford and take their place.

'I cursed three times since last Easter day –
At mass-time once I went to play:
I passed the churchyard one day in haste,
And forgot to pray for my mother's rest.

'I bear no hate against living thing;
But I love my country above my king.
Now, Father! bless me, and let me go
To die, if God has ordained it so.'

The Priest said nought, but a rustling noise
Made the youth look above in wild surprise;
The robes were off, and in scarlet there
Sat a yeoman captain with fiery glare.

With fiery glare and with fury hoarse,
Instead of blessing, he breathed a curse: –
"Twas a good thought, boy, to come here and
          shrive,
For one short hour is your time to live.

'Upon yon river three tenders float,
The Priest's in one, if he isn't shot –
We hold his house for our Lord the King,
And, Amen, say I, may all traitors swing!'

At Geneva Barrack that young man died,
And at Passage they have his body laid.
Good people who live in peace and joy,
Breathe a prayer and a tear for the Croppy Boy.
                    William B McBurney (Carroll Malone),

The Cry of the Dreamer

I am tired of planning and toiling
In the crowded hives of men;
Heart-weary of building and spoiling
And spoiling and building again.
And I long for the dear old river,
Where I dreamed my youth away;
For a dreamer lives forever,
And a toiler dies in a day.

I am sick of the showy seeming
Of a life that is half a lie;
Of the faces lined with scheming
In the throng that hurries by.
From the sleepless thoughts' endeavour,
I would go where the children play;
For a dreamer lives forever,
And a thinker dies in a day.

I can feel no pride but pity
For the burdens the rich endure;
There is nothing sweet in the city
But the patient lives of the poor.
Ah, the little hands too skilful,
And the child-mind choked with weeds!
The daughter's heart grown willful,
And the father's heart that bleeds!

No, No! from the street's rude bustle,
From trophies of mart and stage,
I would fly to the woods' low rustle
And the meadows' kindly page.
Let me dream as of old by the river,
And be loved for the dream alway;
For a dreamer lives forever,
And a toiler dies in a day.

John Boyle O'Reilly

A White Rose

The red rose whispers of passion,
And the white rose breathes of love;
Oh, the red rose is a falcon,
And the white rose is a dove.

But I send you a cream-white rosebud
With a flush on its petal tips;

174

For the love that is purest and sweetest
Has a kiss of desire on the lips.

John Boyle O'Reilly

The Ballad of Reading Gaol

He did not wear his scarlet coat,
For blood and wine are red,
And blood and wine were on his hands
When they found him with the dead,
The poor dead woman whom he loved,
And murdered in her bed.

He walked amongst the Trial Men
In a suit of shabby grey;
A cricket cap was on his head,
And his step seemed light and gay;
But I never saw a man who looked
So wistfully at the day.

I never saw a man who looked
With such a wistful eye
Upon that little tent of blue
Which prisoners call the sky,
And at every drifting cloud that went
With sails of silver by.

I walked with other souls in pain,
Within another ring,
And was wondering if the man had done
A great or little thing,
When a voice behind me whispered low,
'That fellow's got to swing.'

Dear Christ! the very prison walls
Suddenly seemed to reel,
And the sky above my head became

Like a casque of scorching steel;
And, though I was a soul in pain,
My pain I could not feel.

I only knew what hunted thought
Quickened his step, and why
He looked upon the garish day
With such a wistful eye;
The man had killed the thing he loved,
And so he had to die.

Yet each man kills the thing he loves,
By each let this be heard,
Some do it with a bitter look,
Some with a flattering word,
The coward does it with a kiss,
The brave man with a sword!

Some kill their love when they are young,
And some when they are old;
Some strangle with the hands of Lust,
Some with the hands of Gold:
The kindest use a knife, because
The dead so soon grow cold.

Some love too little, some too long,
Some sell, and others buy;
Some do the deed with many tears,
And some without a sigh:
For each man kills the thing he loves,
Yet each man does not die.

He does not die a death of shame
On a day of dark disgrace,
Nor have a noose about his neck,
Nor a cloth upon his face,
Nor drop feet foremost through the floor
Into an empty space.

He does not sit with silent men
Who watch him night and day;
Who watch him when he tries to weep,
And when he tries to pray;
Who watch him lest himself should rob
The prison of its prey.

He does not wake at dawn to see
Dread figures throng his room,
The shivering Chaplain robed in white,
The Sheriff stern with gloom,
And the Governor all in shiny black,
With the yellow face of Doom.

He does not rise in piteous haste
To put on convict-clothes,
While some coarse-mouthed doctor gloats, and
       notes
Each new and nerve-twitched pose,
Fingering a watch whose little ticks
Are like horrible hammer-blows.

He does not know that sickening thirst
That sand one's throat, before
The hangman with his gardener's gloves
Slips through the padded door,
And binds one with three leathern thongs
That the throat may thirst no more.

He does not bend his head to hear
The Burial Office read,
Nor, while the terror of his soul
Tells him he is not dead,
Cross his own coffin, as he moves
Into the hideous shed.

He does not stare upon the air
Through a little roof of glass:
He does not pray with lips of clay

For his agony to pass;
Nor feel upon his shuddering cheek
The kiss of Caiaphas.

II

Six weeks our guardsman walked the yard
In the suit of shabby grey:
His cricket cap was on his head,
And his step seemed light and gay,
But I never saw a man who looked
So wistfully at the day.

I never saw a man who looked
With such a wistful eye
Upon that little tent of blue
Which prisoners call the sky.
And at every wandering cloud that trailed
Its ravelled fleeces by.

He did not wring his hands, as do
Those witless men who dare
To try to rear the changeling Hope
In the cave of black Despair:
He only looked upon the sun,
And drank the morning air.

He did not wring his hands nor weep,
Nor did he peek or pine,
But he drank the air as though it held
Some healthful anodyne;
With open mouth he drank the sun
As though it had been wine!

And I and all the souls in pain,
Who tramped the other ring,
Forgot if we ourselves had done
A great or little thing,
And watched with gaze of dull amaze

The man who had to swing.

And strange it was to see him pass
With step so light and gay,
And strange it was to see him look
So wistfully at the day,
And strange it was to think that he
Had such a debt to pay.

For oak and elm have pleasant leaves
That in the spring-time shoot:
But grim to see is the gallows-tree,
With its adder-bitten root,
And, green or dry, a man must die
Before it bears its fruit.

The loftiest place is that seat of grace
For which all worldlings try:
But who would stand in hempen band
Upon a scaffold high,
And through a murderer's collar take
His last look at the sky?

It is sweet to dance to violins
When Love and Life are fair:
To dance to flutes, to dance to lutes
Is delicate and rare:
But it is not sweet with nimble feet
To dance upon the air!

So with curious eyes and sick surmise
We watched him day by day,
And wondered if each one of us
Would end the self-same way,
For none can tell to what red hell
His sightless soul may stray.

At last the dead man walked no more
Amongst the Trial Men,

And I knew that he was standing up
In the black dock's dreadful pen,
And that never would I see his face
In God's sweet world again.

Like two doomed ships that pass in storm
We had crossed each other's way:
But we made no sign, we said no word,
We had no word to say;
For we did not meet in the holy night,
But in the shameful day.

A prison wall was round us both,
Two outcast men we were:
The world had thrust us from its heart,
And God from out His care:
And the iron gin that waits for Sin
Had caught us in its snare.

III

In Debtor's Yard the stones are hard,
And the dripping wall is high,
So it was there he took the air
Beneath the leaden sky.
And by each side a Warder walked,
For fear the man might die.

Or else he sat with those who watched
His anguish night and day;
Who watched him when he rose to weep,
And when he crouched to pray;
Who watched him lest himself should rob
Their scaffold of its prey.

The Governor was strong upon
The Regulations Act:
The Doctor said that Death was but
A scientific fact:

And twice a day the chaplain called,
And left a little tract.

And twice a day he smoked his pipe,
And drank his quart of beer:
His soul was resolute, and held
No hiding-place for fear;
He often said that he was glad
The hangman's hands were near.

But why he said so strange a thing
No warder dared to ask:
For he to whom a watcher's doom
Is given as his task,
Must set a lock upon his lips,
And make his face a mask.

Or else he might be moved, and try
To comfort or console:
And what should Human Pity do
Pent up in Murderer's Hole?
What word of grace in such a place
Could help a brother's soul?

With slouch and swing around the ring
We trod the Fools' Parade!
We did not care: we knew we were
The Devil's Own Brigade:
And shaven head and feet of lead
Make a merry masquerade.

We tore the tarry rope to shreds
With blunt and bleeding nails:
We rubbed the doors, and scrubbed the floors,
And cleaned the shining rails:
And, rank by rank, we soaped the plank,
And clattered with the pails.

We sewed the sacks, we broke the stones.

We turned the dusty drill:
We banged the tins, and bawled the hymns,
And sweated on the mill:
But in the heart of every man
Terror was lying still.

So still it lay that every day
Crawled like a weed-clogged wave:
And we forgot the bitter lot
That waits for fool and knave,
Till once, as we tramped in from work,
We passed an open grave.

With yawning mouth the yellow hole
Gaped for a living thing;
The very mud cried out for blood
To the thirsty asphalt ring:
And we knew that ere one dawn grew fair
Some prisoner had to swing.

Right in we went, with soul intent
On Death, and Dread and Doom:
The hangman, with his little bag,
Went shuffling through the gloom:
And each man trembled as he crept
Into his numbered tomb.

That night the empty corridors
Were full of forms of Fear,
And up and down the iron town
Stole feet we could not hear,
And through the bars that hide the stars
White faces seemed to peer.

He lay as one who lies and dreams
In a pleasant meadow-land,
And watchers watched him as he slept,
And could not understand
How one could sleep so sweet a sleep

With a hangman close at hand.

But there is no sleep when men must weep
Who never yet have wept:
So we – the fool, the fraud, the knave –
That endless vigil kept,
And through each brain on hands of pain
Another's terror crept.

Alas! it is a fearful thing
To feel another's guilt!
For, right within, the sword of Sin
Pierced to its poisoned hilt,
And as molten lead were the tears we shed
For the blood we had not spilt.

The Warders with their shoes of felt
Crept by each padlocked door,
And peeped and saw, with eyes of awe,
Grey figures on the floor,
And wondered why men knelt to pray
Who never prayed before.

All through the night we knelt and prayed,
Mad mourners of a corse!
The troubled plumes of midnight were
The plumes upon a hearse:
And bitter wine upon a sponge
Was the savor of Remorse.

The grey cock crew, the red cock crew,
But never came the day:
And crooked shapes of Terror crouched,
In the corners where they lay:
And each evil sprite that walks by night
Before us seemed to play.

They glided past, they glided fast,
Like travellers through a mist:

They mocked the moon in a rigadoon
Of delicate turn and twist,
And with formal pace and loathsome grace
The phantoms kept their tryst.

With mop and mow we saw them go,
Slim shadows hand in hand:
About, about, in ghostly rout
They trod a saraband:
And the damned grotesques made arabesques,
Like the wind upon the sand!

With the pirouettes of marionettes,
They tripped on pointed tread:
But with flutes of Fear they filled the ear,
As their grisly masque they led,
And loud they sang, and long they sang,
For they sang to wake the dead.

'Oho!' they cried, 'The world is wide,
But fettered limbs go lame!
And once, or twice, to throw the dice
Is a gentlemanly game;
But he does not win who plays with sin
In the secret house of shame.'

No things of air these antics were,
That frolicked with such glee:
To men whose lives were held in gyves,
And whose feet might not go free,
Ah! wounds of Christ! they were living things,
Most terrible to see.

Around, around, they waltzed and wound;
Some wheeled in smirking pairs;
With the mincing step of a demirep
Some sidled up the stairs:
And with subtle sneer, and fawning leer,
Each helped us at our prayers.

The morning wind began to moan,
But still the night went on:
Through its giant loom the web of gloom
Crept till each thread was spun:
And, as we prayed, we grew afraid
Of the Justice of the Sun.

The moaning wind went wandering round
The weeping prison-wall:
Till like a wheel of turning steel
We felt the minutes crawl:
O moaning wind! what had we done
To have such a seneschal?

At last I saw the shadowed bars,
Like a lattice wrought in lead,
Move right across the whitewashed wall
That faced my three-plank bed,
And I knew that somewhere in the world
God's dreadful dawn was red.

At six o'clock we cleaned our cells,
At seven all was still,
But the sough and swing of a mighty wing
The prison seemed to fill,
For the Lord of Death with icy breath
Had entered in to kill.

He did not pass in purple pomp,
Nor ride a moon-white steed.
Three yards of cord and a sliding board
Are all the gallows' need:
So with rope of shame the Herald came
To do the secret deed.

We were as men who through a fen
Of filthy darkness grope:
We did not dare to breathe a prayer,
Or to give our anguish scope:

Something was dead in each of us,
And what was dead was Hope.

For Man's grim Justice goes its way,
And will not swerve aside:
It slays the weak, it slays the strong,
It has a deadly stride:
With iron heel it slays the strong,
The monstrous parricide!

We waited for the stroke of eight:
Each tongue was thick with thirst:
For the stroke of eight is the stroke of Fate
That makes a man accursed,
And Fate will use a running noose
For the best man and the worst.

We had no other thing to do,
Save to wait for the sign to come:
So, like things of stone in a valley lone,
Quiet we sat and dumb:
But each man's heart beat thick and quick,
Like a madman on a drum!

With sudden shock the prison clock
Smote on the shivering air,
And from all the gaol rose up a wail
Of impotent despair,
Like the sound that frightened marshes hear
From some leper in his lair.

And as one sees most fearful things
In the crystal of a dream,
We saw the greasy hempen rope
Hooked to the blackened beam,
And heard the prayer the hangman's snare
Strangled into a scream.

And all the woe that moved him so

That he gave that bitter cry,
And the wild regrets, and the bloody sweats,
None knew so well as I:
For he who lives more lives than one
More deaths than one must die.

IV

There is no chapel on the day
On which they hang a man:
The Chaplain's heart is much too sick,
Or his face is far too wan,
Or there is that written in his eyes
Which none should look upon.

So they kept us close till nigh on noon,
And then they rang the bell,
And the Warders with their jingling keys
Opened each listening cell,
And down the iron stair we tramped,
Each from his separate Hell.

Out into God's sweet air we went,
But not in wonted way,
For this man's face was white with fear,
And that man's face was gray,
And I never saw sad men who looked
So wistfully at the day.

I never saw sad men who looked
With such a wistful eye
Upon that little tent of blue
We prisoners call the sky,
And at every careless cloud that passed
In happy freedom by.

But there were those amongst us all
Who walked with downcast head,
And knew that, had each got his due,

They should have died instead:
He had but killed a thing that lived,
Whilst they had killed the dead.

For he who sins a second time
Wakes a dead soul to pain,
And draws it from its spotted shroud,
And makes it bleed again,
And makes it bleed great gouts of blood,
And makes it bleed in vain!

Like ape or clown, in monstrous garb
With crooked arrows starred,
Silently we went round and round
The slippery asphalt yard;
Silently we went round and round,
And no man spoke a word.

Silently we went round and round,
And through each hollow mind
The Memory of dreadful things
Rushed like a dreadful wind,
And Horror stalked before each man,
And Terror crept behind.

The Warders strutted up and down,
And kept their herd of brutes,
Their uniforms were spick and span,
And they wore their Sunday suits,
But we knew the work they had been at,
By the quicklime on their boots.

For where a grave had opened wide,
There was no grave at all:
Only a stretch of mud and sand
By the hideous prison-wall,
And a little heap of burning lime,
That the man should have his pall.

For he has a pall, this wretched man,
Such as few men can claim:
Deep down below a prison-yard,
Naked for greater shame,
He lies, with fetters on each foot,
Wrapt in a sheet of flame!

And all the while the burning lime
Eats flesh and bone away;
It eats the brittle bone by night,
And the soft flesh by day,
It eats the flesh and bone by turns,
But it eats the heart away.

For three long years they will not sow
Or root or seedling there:
For three long years the unblessed spot
Will sterile be and bare,
And look upon the wondering sky
With unreproachful stare.

They think a murderer's heart would taint
Each simple seed they sow.
It is not true! God's kindly earth
Is kindlier than men know,
And the red rose would but blow more red,
The white rose whiter blow.

Out of his mouth a red, red rose!
Out of his heart a white!
For who can say by what strange way,
Christ brings His will to light,
Since the barren staff the pilgrim bore
Bloomed in the great Pope's sight?

But neither milk-white rose nor red
May bloom in prison air;
The shard, the pebble, and the flint,
Are what they give us there:

For flowers have been known to heal
A common man's despair.

So never will wine-red rose or white,
Petal by petal, fall
On that stretch of mud and sand that lies
By the hideous prison-wall,
To tell the men who tramp the yard
That God's son died for all.

Yet though the hideous prison-wall
Still hems him round and round,
And a spirit may not walk by night
That is with fetters bound,
And a spirit may but weep that lies
In such unholy ground.

He is at peace – this wretched man –
At peace, or will be soon:
There is no thing to make him mad,
Nor does Terror walk at noon,
For the lampless Earth in which he lies
Has neither Sun nor Moon.

They hanged him as a beast is hanged:
They did not even toll
A requiem that might have brought
Rest to his startled soul,
But hurriedly they took him out,
And hid him in a hole.

They stripped him of his canvas clothes,
And gave him to the flies;
They mocked the swollen purple throat,
And the stark and staring eyes;
And with laughter loud they heaped the shroud
In which their convict lies.

The Chaplain would not kneel to pray

By this dishonoured grave:
Nor mark it with that blessed Cross
That Christ for sinners gave,
Because the man was one of those
Whom Christ came down to save.

Yet all is well; he has but passed
To Life's appointed bourne:
And alien tears will fill for him
Pity's long-broken urn,
For his mourner's will be outcast men,
And outcasts always mourn.

V

I know not whether Laws be right,
Or whether Laws be wrong;
All that we know who lie in gaol
Is that the wall is strong;
And that each day is like a year,
A year whose days are long.

But this I know, that every Law
That men have made for Man,
Since first Man took his brother's life,
And the sad world began,
But straws the wheat and saves the chaff
With a most evil fan.

This too I know – and wise it were
If each should know the same –
That every prison that men build
Is built with bricks of shame,
And bound with bars lest Christ should see
How men their brothers maim.

With bars they blur the gracious moon,
And blind the goodly sun:
And they do well to hide their Hell,

For in it things are done
That Son of God nor Son of Man
Ever should look upon!

The vilest deeds like poison weeds
Bloom well in prison-air:
It is only what is good in Man
That wastes and withers there:
Pale anguish keeps the heavy gate,
And the Warder is Despair.

For they starve the little frightened child
Till it weeps both night and day:
And they scourge the weak, and flog the fool,
And gibe the old and gray,
And some grow mad, and all grow bad,
And none a word may say.

Each narrow cell in which we dwell
Is a foul and dark latrine.
And the fetid breath of living Death
Chokes up each grated screen,
And all, but Lust, is turned to dust
In Humanity's machine.

The brackish water that we drink
Creeps with a loathsome slime,
And the bitter bread they weigh in scales
Is full of chalk and lime,
And Sleep will not lie down, but walks
Wild-eyed, and dries to Time.

But though lean Hunger and green Thirst
Like asp with adder fight,
We have little care of prison fare,
For what chills and kills outright
Is that every stone one lifts by day
Becomes one's heart by night.

With midnight always in one's heart,
And twilight in one's cell,
We turn the crank, or tear the rope,
Each in his separate Hell,
And the silence is more awful far
Than the sound of a brazen bell.

And never a human voice comes near
To speak a gentle word:
And the eye that watches through the door
Is pitiless and hard:
And by all forgot, we rot and rot,
With soul and body marred.

And thus we rust Life's iron chain
Degraded and alone:
And some men curse, and some men weep,
And some men make no moan:
But God's eternal laws are kind
And break the heart of stone.

And every human heart that breaks,
In prison-cell or yard,
Is as that broken box that gave
Its treasure to the Lord,
And filled the unclean leper's house
With the scent of costliest nard.

Ah! happy they whose hearts can break
And peace of pardon win!
How else may man make straight his plan
And cleanse his soul from Sin?
How else but through a broken heart
May Lord Christ enter in?

And he of the swollen purple throat,
And the stark and staring eyes
Waits for the holy hands that took
The Thief to Paradise;

And a broken and a contrite heart
The Lord will not despise.

The man in red who reads the law
Gave him three weeks of life,
Three little weeks in which to heal
His soul of his soul's strife,
And cleanse from every blot of blood
The hand that held the knife.

And with tears of blood he cleansed the hand,
The hand that held the steel:
For only blood can wipe out blood,
And only tears can heal:
And the crimson stain that was of Cain
Became Christ's snow-white seal.

VI

In Reading gaol by Reading town
There is a pit of shame,
And in it lies a wretched man
Eaten by teeth of flame,
In a burning winding-sheet he lies,
And his grave has got no name.

And there, till Christ call forth the dead,
In silence let him lie:
No need to waste the foolish tear,
Or heave the windy sigh:
The man had killed the thing he loved,
And so he had to die.

And all men kill the thing they love,
By all let this be heard,
Some do it with a bitter look,
Some with a flattering word,
The coward does it with a kiss,
The brave man with a sword!

Oscar Wilde

Dublin Girl, Mountjoy 1984

(do Nuala)

I dreamt it all, from end to end, the carriageway,
The rivulet behind the dairy streaked with crystal,
A steel moon glinting in a guttered stream of rain,
And the steep hill that I would crest to find her,
My child asleep in my old bedroom beside my sister.

I dreamt it all, and when I woke, furtive girls
Were clambering onto the bars of the windows,
White shapes waving against the sky's uniform,
Praying for hands to reply from the men's cells
Before screws broke up the vigil of handkerchiefs.

I dreamt it all, the times I swore, never again
To walk that carriageway, a rivulet of fear glowing
In my veins until I shivered within its aftertaste
And hid with my child in the closed down factory
Where my brain snapped like a brittle fingernail.

I dreamt it all, the longing to touch, the seance
In the cell when we screamed at the picture falling,
The warmth of circled hands after the numbing glass
Between my child and me, a warder following her
  words
To be rationed out and lived off for days afterwards.

I dreamt of you, who means all to me, my daughter,
How we might run to that carriageway by the rivulet,
And when I woke a blue pupil was patrolling my sleep,
Jailing my dreams into the empty orbit of its world
Narrowed down to a spyhole, a globed eyelid closing.

Dermot Bolger

The Witch

Margaret Grady – I fear she will burn –

Charmed the butter off my churn;
'Tis I would know it the wide world over,
Yellow as saffron, scented with clover.

At Omagh market the witch displayed it:
Ill she had gathered, ill she had made it.
Hid in my cloak's hood, one glance I threw it,
Passed on smiling; my troth! I knew it!

Sheila, the kindest cow in the parish,
Mild and silken, and good to cherish,
Shame her own gold butter should leave her
To enrich the milk of a low-bred heifer!

I said not Yea or Nay to the mocker,
But called the fairy-man over from Augher;
Like a russet he is that's withered,
Bent in two with his wisdom gathered.

He touched the butter, he peered and pondered,
And crooned strange rhymes while I watched and
    wondered:
Then he drew me out through the gloaming
O'er the fields where the mist was coming.

He bewitched me so that I know not
Where they may grow, where they may grow not;
Those witch-hazels he plucked and plaited,
Crooning on while the twigs he mated.

There's the wreath on the church-dash yonder.
All the neighbours view it with wonder;
And 'spite of Father Tom I avow it
The yield is doubled since that came to it.

I bless the fairy-man though he be evil;
Yet fairy-spells come not from the devil;
And Margaret Grady – I fear she will burn –
I do forgive her, with hate and scorn.

Katherine Tynan Hinkson

Buying Winkles

My mother would spare me sixpence and say,
'Hurry up now and don't be talking to strange
men on the way.' I'd dash from the ghosts
on the stairs where the bulb had blown
out into Gardiner Street, all relief.
A bonus if the moon was in the strip of the sky
between the tall houses, or stars out,
but even in rain I was happy – the winkles
would be wet and glisten blue like little
night skies themselves. I'd hold the tanner tight
and jump every crack in the pavement,
I'd wave up to women at sills or those
lingering in doorways and weave a glad path through
men heading out for the night.

She'd be sitting outside the Rosebowl Bar
on an orange-crate, a pram loaded
with pails of winkles before her.
When the bar doors swung open they'd leak
the smell of men together with drink
and I'd see light in golden mirrors.
I envied each soul in the hot interior.

I'd ask her again to show me the right way
to do *it*. She'd take a pin from her shawl –
'Open the eyelid. So. Stick it in
till you feel a grip, then slither him out.
Gently, mind.' The sweetest extra winkle
that brought the sea to me.
'Tell yer Ma I picked them fresh this morning.'

I'd bear the newspaper twists
bulging fat with winkles
proudly home, like torches.

Paula Meehan

The Little Waves of Breffny

The grand road from the mountain goes shining to the sea,
And there is traffic in it and many a horse and cart,
But the little roads of Cloonagh are dearer far to me,
And the little roads of Cloonagh go rambling through my
      heart.

A great storm from the ocean goes shouting o'er the hill,
And there is glory in it and terror on the wind,
But the haunted air of twilight is very strange and still,
And the little winds of twilight are dearer to my mind.

The great waves of the Atlantic sweep storming on the way,
Shining green and silver with the hidden herring shoal,
But the Little Waves of Breffny have drenched my heart in
      spray.
And the Little Waves of Breffny go stumbling through my
      soul.

Eva Gore-Booth

I will go with my Father a-Ploughing

I will go with my father a-ploughing
To the green field by the sea,
And the rooks and the crows and the seagulls
Will come flocking after me.
I will sing to the patient horses
With the lark in the white of the air,
And my father will sing the plough-song
That blesses the cleaving share.

I will go with my father a-sowing
To the red field by the sea,
And the rooks and the gulls and the starlings
Will come flocking after me.

198

I will sing to the striding sowers
With the finch on the flowering sloe,
And my father will sing the seed-song
That only the wise men know.

I will go with my father a-reaping
To the brown field by the sea,
And the geese and the crows and the children
Will come flocking after me.
I will sing to the weary reapers
With the wren in the heat of the sun,
And my father will sing the scythe-song
That joys for the harvest done.

Joseph Campbell

To my Daughter Betty, the Gift of God

In wiser days, my darling rosebud, blown
To beauty proud as was your mother's prime,
In that desired, delayed, incredible time,
You'll ask why I abandoned you, my own,
And the dear heart that was your baby throne,
To dice with death. And oh! they'll give you rhyme
And reason: some will call the thing sublime,
And some decry it in a knowing tone.
So here, while the mad guns curse overhead,
And tired men sigh with mud for couch and floor,
Know that we fools, now with the foolish dead,
Died not for flag, nor King, nor Emperor –
But for a dream, born in a herdman's shed,
And for the secret Scripture of the poor.

Thomas M Kettle

The Dead at Clonmacnois

In a quiet water'd land, a land of roses,

Stands St Kieran's city fair:
And the warriors of Erin in their famous generations
Slumber there.

There beneath the dewy hillside sleep the noblest
Of the clan of Conn,
Each below his stone with name in branching Ogham
And the sacred knot thereon.

There they laid to rest the seven Kings of Tara,
There the sons of Cairbré sleep –
Battle-banners of the Gael, that in Kieran's plain of
    crosses
Now their final hosting keep.

And in Clonmacnois they laid the men of Teffia,
And right many a lord of Breagh;
Deep the sod above Clan Creidé and Clan Conaill,
Kind in hall and fierce in fray.

Many and many a son of Conn, the Hundred-Fighter,
In the red earth lies at rest;
Many a blue eye of Clan Colman the turf covers,
Many a swan-white breast.

Angus O'Gillan – Translated by T W Rolleston

Ballad to a Traditional Refrain

Red brick in the suburbs, white horse on the wall,
Eyetalian marbles in the City Hall:
O stranger from England, why stand so aghast?
May the Lord in His mercy be kind to Belfast.

This jewel that houses our hopes and our fears
Was knocked up from the swamp in the last hundred
    years;
But the last shall be first and the first shall be last:

May the Lord in His mercy be kind to Belfast.

We swore by King William there'd never be seen
An All-Irish Parliament at College Green,
So at Stormont we're nailing the flag to the mast:
May the Lord in His mercy be kind to Belfast.

O the bricks they will bleed and the rain it will weep,
And the damp Lagan fog lull the city to sleep;
It's to hell with the future and live on the past:
May the Lord in His Mercy be kind to Belfast.

Maurice Craig

Wounds

Here are two pictures from my father's head –
I have kept them like secrets up until now:
First, the Ulster Division at the Somme
Going over the top with 'Fuck the pope!'
'No Surrender!': a boy about to die,
Screaming 'Give 'em one for the Shankill!'
'Wilder than Gurkhas' were my father's words
Of admiration and bewilderment.
Next comes the London–Scottish padre
Resettling kilts with his swagger-stick,
With a stylish backhand and a prayer.
Over a landscape of dead buttocks
My father followed him for fifty years.
At last, a belated casualty,
He said – lead traces flaring till they hurt –
'I am dying for King and Country, slowly.'
I touched his hand, his thin head I touched.

Now, with military honours of a kind,
With his badges, his medals like rainbows,
His spinning compass, I bury beside him
Three teenage soldiers, bellies full of

Bullets and Irish beer, their flies undone.
A packet of woodbines I throw in,
A lucifer, the Sacred Heart of Jesus
Paralysed as heavy guns put out
The night-light in a nursery for ever;
Also a bus-conductor's uniform –
He collapsed beside his carpet-slippers
Without a murmur, shot through the head
By a shivering boy who wandered in
Before they could turn the television down
Or tidy away the supper dishes.
To the children, to a bewildered wife,
I think 'Sorry Missus' was what he said.

Michael Longley

The Wayfarer

The beauty of the world hath made me sad,
This beauty that will pass;
Sometimes my heart hath shaken with great joy
To see a leaping squirrel in a tree,
Or a red lady-bird upon a stalk,
Or little rabbits in a field at evening,
Lit by a slanting sun,
Or some green hill where shadows drifted by
Some quiet hill where mountainy man hath sown
And soon would reap; near to the gate of Heaven;
Or children with bare feet upon the sands
Of some ebbed sea, or playing on the streets
Of little towns in Connacht,
Things young and happy.
And then my heart hath told me:
These will pass,
Will pass and change, will die and be no more,
Things bright and green, things young and happy;
And I have gone upon my way
Sorrowful.

Patrick Pearse

Party Shrine

My father is clearing the first Party shrine:
it is the summer of Sixty-six.
He hates physical work and everything
that keeps him from the protection racket
of crosswords and history books.
But the rest of the Committee
has been drunk since the Jubilee
and can't break the spell of itself.

Weeds know nothing about the Party
or how it emerged, genie-like,
out of an abandoned shell case.
The weeds and their friends the shitting
pigeons want to bury this shrine
in a single summer.
I am holding the shovel for my father
while he reads inscriptions on brass:
sixteen golden names of the Party,
the twenty-six grammatical flaws.

Thomas McCarthy

Letter to a British Soldier on Irish Soil

I

Soldier
You did not ask to come here
We know that.
You obey orders
We know that.
You have a wife
A sweetheart
A mother

We know that.
And you have children
We know that too.
But, Soldier
Where you stand
There is death.
Where you walk
There is a burning wound.
Where you sleep
There is no peace
And the earth heaves
Through a nightmare of blood.
Soldier
When you die
The dogs will bury you.

II

When you came to this land
You said you came to understand.
Soldier, we are tired of your understanding.
Tired of British troops on Irish soil
Tired of your knock upon the door
Tired of the rifle butt on the head
Tired of the jails, the gas, the beatings
In dark corners.
Soldier
We are tired of the peace you bring
To Irish bones,
Tired of the bombs exploding in our homes
Tired of the rubble growing in the streets
Tired of the deaths of our friends
Tired of the tears and the funerals –
Those endless, endless funerals.
Soldier
When you came to this land
You said you came to understand.
Is this your understanding?

III

We dream here.
We dream that this land
Is our land.
That one day
Catholic and Protestant
Believer and Non-believer
Will stand here
And dream
As Irishmen.
We dream
Of a green land
Without death.
A new silence descending
A silence of peace.
And this dream
We dream, Soldier
Without you.
That is our understanding.

IV

Go home, Soldier.
Your presence here
Destroys the air
Your smile disfigures us.
Go home, Soldier
Before we send you home
Dead.

Patrick Galvin

Protestant Boys

Tell me, friends, why are we met here?
Why thus assembled, ye Protestant Boys?

Do mirth and good liquor, good humour, good
        cheer,
Call us to share of festivity's joys?
Oh, no! 'tis the cause
Of king, freedom, and laws,
That calls loyal Protestants now to unite;
And Orange and Blue,
Ever faithful and true,
Our king shall support, and sedition affright.

Great spirit of William! from heaven look down,
And breathe in our heart's our forefathers' fire –
Teach us to rival their glorious renown,
From Papist or Frenchman ne'er to retire.
Jacobin – Jacobite –
Against all to unite,
Who dare to assail our sovereign's throne?
For Orange and Blue
Will be faithful and true,
And Protestant loyalty ever be shown.

In that loyalty proud let us ever remain,
Bound together in truth and religion's pure band;
Nor honour's fair cause with foul bigotry stain,
Since in courage and justice supported we stand
So heaven shall smile
On our emerald isle,
And lead us to conquest again and again;
While Papists shall prove
Our brotherly love; –
We hate them as masters – we love them as men.

By the deeds of their fathers to glory inspired,
Our Protestant heroes shall combat the foe;
Hearts with true honor and loyalty fired,
Intrepid, undaunted, to conquest will go.
In Orange and Blue,
Still faithful and true,
The soul-stirring music of glory they'll sing;

The shades of the Boyne
In the chorus will join,
And the welkin re-echo with God save the king.

Anonymous

The Lundys Letter

You staged the ultimate *coup de grace*
for the Union's son turned republican.
I can see you shivering in the cold
of an East Belfast morning, outside
school, the bikes upended, the quad
blown by a dusty wind, and rows of
windows, some cellophaned, gaze
back at the encroaching estate.

Even your voice was different, haughty
we thought, the grand dismissive way
you demonstrated learning, or in *Tartuffe*
worked a subtle authority over our
ragged rebelliousness that we
should sit through such performances
of high art in a secondary school!

A generation growing but no hard-hats
for us or the miserable one-step up
a slippery ladder to civil service.
I don't know where you went; we got
lost in London or tried our wings
on an amalgam of desperate love
and politics at the new university.

And then the next time it was a warm
summer's day at Woolworth's when
the ground shook and a tailor's dummy
crashed through sheets of glass,
and there was hardly time to ask
how you were keeping as shoe-boxes flew

all over the place and the bomb
finished its work on down High Street.

Walking to the Dole, the clang in my ears
of sirens and trampling feet,
it was another lock of years
before I saw you in a pub by chance,
barely the same, chose not to recognise –
I only bear witness now to what was,
and hear your prefect's voice of derision
shout to a smoking third-form class.

Gerald Dawe

Claudy
For Harry Barton – a Song

The Sperrins surround it, the Faughan flows by,
at each end of Main Street the hills and the sky,
the small town of Claudy at ease in the sun
last July in the morning, a new day begun.

How peaceful and pretty if the moment could stop,
McIlhenny is straightening things in his shop,
and his wife is outside serving petrol, and then
a girl takes a cloth to a big window pane.

And McCloskey is taking the weight off his feet,
and McClelland and Miller are sweeping the street,
and, delivering milk at the Beaufort Hotel,
young Temple's enjoying his first job quite well.

And Mrs McLaughlin is scrubbing her floor,
and Artie Hone's crossing the street to a door,
and Mrs Brown, looking around for her cat,
goes off up an entry – what's strange about that?

Not much – but before she comes back to the road

that strange car parked outside her house will explode,
and all of the people I've mentioned outside
will be waiting to die or already have died.

An explosion too loud for your eardrums to bear,
and young children squealing like pigs in the square,
and all faces chalk-white and streaked with bright red,
and the glass and the dust and the terrible dead.

For an old lady's legs are ripped off, and the head
of a man's hanging open, and still he's not dead.
He is screaming for mercy, and his son stands and stares
and stares, and then suddenly, quick, disappears.

And Christ, little Katherine Aiken is dead,
and Mrs McLaughlin is pierced through the head.
Meanwhile to Dungiven the killers have gone,
and they're finding it hard to get through on the phone.

James Simmons

The Mystery

I am the wind which breathes upon the sea,
I am the wave of the ocean,
I am the murmur of the billows,
I am the ox of the seven combats,
I am the vulture upon the rocks,
I am a beam of the sun,
I am the fairest of plants,
I am a wild boar in valour,
I am a salmon in the water,
I am a lake in the plain,
I am a word of science,
I am the point of the lance of battle,
I am the God who created in the head the fire.
Who is it who throws light into the meeting on the
            mountain?

Who announces the ages of the moon?
Who teaches the place where couches the sun?
                    (If not I)
                              Amergin – Translated by Douglas Hyde

The Killing of Dreams

They are encoded and are the past,
cannot be implanted in souls or brains,
not by the learning of lists
nor by learning definitions of names:
this is injecting the dream vaccine
which does not make better but makes die
the entities of the mist
that wait in the hollows of our heads.
We graft the hobbled dream
onto the inbuilt dream:
acid on alkali.
Some of us, afraid we lack
the findings of the analyst,
inject the vaccine in
the sanctum of the heart
only to find that it rejects
the artificial part
and leaves us dreamless in the dark.
This, the learning of lists,
this taking water to the well,
this planting of waterweed in streams,
this addiction to the fix
developed by the alchemists of print –
this is the killing of dreams.

                              Michael Hartnett

Peace

And sometimes I am sorry when the grass

Is growing over the stones in quiet hollows
And the cocksfoot leans across the rutted cart-pass
That I am not the voice of country fellows
Who now are standing by some headland talking
Of turnips and potatoes or young corn
Or turf banks stripped for victory.
Here peace is still hawking
His coloured combs and scarves and beads of horn.

Upon a headland by a whiny hedge
A hare sits looking down a leaf-lapped furrow,
There's an old plough upside-down on a weedy ridge
And someone is shouldering home a saddle-harrow.
Out of that childhood country what fools climb
To fight with tyrants Love and Life and Time?

Patrick Kavanagh

Acknowledgements

Thanks are due to the following for permission to reprint the material indicated: 'Innocence' and 'Peace' by Patrick Kavanagh, by permission of the trustees of the Estate of Patrick Kavanagh, c/o Peter Fallon, Literary Agent, Loughcrew, Oldcastle, Co. Meath; The Gallery Press and Paula Meehan, James Simmons, Michael Hartnett, Sean Dunne, John Montague, Gerald Dawe for – 'Buying Winkles' and 'Return and No Blame' by Paula Meehan from *The Man Who was Marked by Winter*, (1991), 'Claudy' by James Simmons from *Poems 1956–1986*, (1986), 'The Killing of Dreams' by Michael Hartnett from *The Killing of Dreams*, © 1992, 'The Lundys Letter' by Gerald Dawe from *Sunday School*, © 1991, 'Throwing the Beads' by Sean Dunne from *The Sheltered Nest*, © 1992, 'Like Dolmens Round My Childhood the Old People' by John Montague from *New Selected Poems*, © 1989; Faber and Faber Ltd – 'Seals at High Tide' by Richard Murphy from *New Selected Poems*, extract from 'Autumn Journal, XVI' from *The Collected Poems of Louis MacNeice* edited by E. R. Dodd, 'Poem' by Seamus Heaney from *Death of a Naturalist*; The Blackstaff Press – 'Ulster Names' by John Hewitt from *The Collected Poems of John Hewitt*, 'The Jewish Bride' by Paul Durcan; Martin, Brian and O'Keeffe – 'Letter to a British Soldier on Irish Soil' by Patrick Galvin; Reprinted by permission of Bloodaxe Books Ltd from *Hail! Madam Jazz* ['Between'] by Micheal O'Siadhail (Bloodaxe Books, 1992); Raven Arts Press – 'My Life, My Voice, My Story' by Davoren Hanna from *Not Common Speech*; Martin Secker & Warburg Ltd – 'Wounds' by Michael Longley from *Poems 1963–1983*, ; © Derek Mahon 1979. ['A Disused Shed in Co. Wexford'] Reprinted from *Poems 1962–1978* by Derek Mahon (1979) by permission of Oxford University Press; Carcanet Press Ltd – 'The Journey's End' and 'Envoi' by Eavan Boland from *Selected Poems*; A. P. Watt Ltd on behalf of Wyn Fisher for 'An Ulsterman' by Lynn Doyle; Anvil Press Poetry Ltd – 'Party Shrine' by Thomas McCarthy from *The Non-Aligned Storyteller* by Thomas McCarthy and published by Anvil Press Poetry in 1984; John B. Keane for 'The Street'; Rosemarie Rowley for 'Fair and Forty' from *The Broken Pledge* published by Martello Publications (Dublin 1985); Maurice Craig for 'Ballad to a Traditional Refrain'; Joan Rea for 'The Man from God-Knows-Where' by Florence Wilson; Katie Donovan for 'First Autumn Night'; Dermot Bolger for 'Dublin Girl'; R Dardis Clarke, 21 Pleasants Street, Dublin 8 for 'The Redemptorist' by Austin Clarke; Simon D Campbell for 'I will go with my Father a-Ploughing' by Joseph Campbell; Douglas Sealy for Douglas Hyde's translation of 'The Mystery' by Amergin; Mercier Press and Cosslett Ó Cuinn for his translation of 'The Midnight Court' by Brian Merriman.

Every effort has been made to trace the owners of copyright material and it is hoped that no copyright has been infringed. If we have inadvertently infringed any copyright we apologise and will make the necessary correction at the first opportunity.

LOVE OF IRELAND: POEMS FROM THE IRISH

Brendan Kennelly

Love of Ireland is a magical collection of translations from the Irish by one of Ireland's leading poets, Brendan Kennelly. Here he has captured all of the spontaneity, candour, freshness and emotional fullness of Irish poetry.

Love of Ireland includes translations of many well-known poems including 'The Old Woman of Beare', 'Kate of Gornavilla', 'A Cry for Art O'Leary' and the beautiful address to 'Mary'.

MOLONEY UP AND AT IT
Brendan Kennelly

Moloney Up and At It is a collection of comic poems with the central character, Moloney, who tells of his experiences of, for the most part, sex and death. The language of the poems is that of the south-west of Ireland, of north Kerry in particular. Brendan Kennelly's intention was to capture the easy, bawdy humour, the candid speech and the fluent power of narrative of so many of the men and women he heard telling stories.

BALLADS OF A BOGMAN

Sigerson Clifford

Almost invariably Sigerson Clifford has set his word pictures against the mountain backdrop that edges Dingle Bay from the Laune to the Inney. To visit his Kerry is to go with him along the heathery pathways above Cahirciveen, or to sit with him in the cosy pub. With a rare sense of intimacy he will take you on bare feet through the dew-wet grass of sloping fields before the morning sun tops the shoulder of one of his mountains, or set you down in the scent of the smouldering turf under low rafters as darkly brown as the stout in your glass. In these poems Sigerson Clifford has caught and held the witchery of Kerry.

AROUND THE BOREE LOG
and other verses

John O'Brien

Around the Boree Log is verse that is simple and sincere and lit with kindly understanding of the lives it chronicles.

> *For when the Holy Morning strung*
> *Its beads upon the grass,*
> *You'd see us driving – old and young –*
> *The tall white graceful trees among,*
> *On every road to Mass.*

DÁNTA BAN
Poems of Irish Women – Early and Modern
Selected and translated by P. L. Henry

DÁNTA BAN: POEMS OF IRISH WOMEN is an historical anthology reflecting the social status and role of women from the earliest times to the present.

Old Irish lyric poetry stands at the fountainhead of vernacular poetry in Europe and many celebrated Old Irish lyrics and hymns were found in the monasteries of Europe in the wake of Irish pilgrim monks. This anthology enables us to compare contemporary lyrics with those of the founders of the tradition long ago.

Poets like Máire Mhac an tSaoi, Nuala Ní Dhomhnaill and many others are included in the book. A useful feature is that Professor Henry's translations are placed alongside the original Irish versions.

FORBHAIS DROMA DÁMHGHÁIRE
The Siege of Knocklong
Seán ó Duinn

Originally part of *The Book of Lismore* this ancient Irish epic (which could be called the *Táin* of Munster) is a marvellous story of magic and fantasy, political influence and vengeance, with a wealth of place-names and curious traditions. The story concerns the march of the high-king Cormac MacAirt, his army and druids, from Tara into Munster for the purpose of forcing Fiacha, King of Munster, to pay taxes.

A Dual-Language Book

THE MIDNIGHT COURT
A new translation by Patrick C. Power

This is a racy, word-rich, bawdy poem – full of uncompromising language and attitudes which have earned it increasing admiration and popularity since it was first composed by Brian Merriman in 1780. The bachelor uninterested in marriage and the aged bone-cold married man, the spouse-hunting lady and the dissatisfied spinster; the celebration of a woman's right to sex and marriage; disapproval of clerical celibacy – all these elements form part of *The Midnight Court*.

A Dual-Language Book

MY VILLAGE – MY WORLD
John M. Feehan

My Village – My World is a fascinating account of ordinary people in the countryside. It depicts a way of life that took thousands of years to evolve and mature and was destroyed in a single generation. As John M. Feehan says 'Nobody famous ever came from our village. None of its inhabitants ever achieved great public acclaim ... The people of our village could be described in government statistics as unskilled. That would be a false description. They were all highly skilled, whether in constructing privies or making coffins, digging drains or cutting hedges, droving cattle or tending to stallions ... I do not want to paint a picture of an idyllic village like Goldsmith's phony one. We had our sinners as well as our saints ...'